Pegge Samuel

An Essay on the Coins of Cunobelin

In an Epistle to the Right Reverend the Lord Bishop of Carlisle

Pegge Samuel

An Essay on the Coins of Cunobelin
In an Epistle to the Right Reverend the Lord Bishop of Carlisle

ISBN/EAN: 9783337136697

Printed in Europe, USA, Canada, Australia, Japan

Cover: Foto ©ninafisch / pixelio.de

More available books at **www.hansebooks.com**

AN ESSAY ON THE COINS OF CUNOBELIN:

IN AN EPISTLE

To the Right Reverend the Lord Bishop of CARLISLE,
President of the Society of Antiquaries;

WHEREIN

This Noble Set of COINS is classed, and appropriated to our
BRITISH KING upon rational Grounds;

The Opinions of the Antiquaries on the Word TASCIA are examined
and refuted, and a more probable one proposed;

The COINS are illustrated in a short Commentary;

And the various Uses that may be made of them, in elucidating the Antiquities of this Island
and many Passages of the Classics, are briefly pointed out.

Two Plates are prefixed, wherein all the COINS are collected together in their respective Classes

---

By SAMUEL PEGGE, A. M.

——— "Servit collecta Pecunia." ———

To the whole is subjoined,
A Dissertation on the Seat of the CORITANI;
Addressed to MATTHEW DUANE, Esq; F. S. A. and F. R. S.

LONDON:
Printed for WILLIAM BOWYER, in White Fryars. M DCC LXVI.

ADVERTISEMENT.

THE author of this epistle has the greatest regard imaginable for his friends Mr. Wise and Dr. Pettingal, being thoroughly sensible of their exquisite and extensive learning; for, as we antiquaries of the lower forms are blessed with no large portion of it, those who sit on a higher bench, and are possessed of an uncommon share, are the more to be valued and esteemed. 'Tis much for the honour of the society it should be so. These gentlemen have displayed, both of them, a large fund of erudition in their respective dissertations: This is a concession no person of common candour can refuse to make; but, nevertheless, as it is the basis of the Antiquary Society to admit a modest and laudable freedom of debate (and indeed the subject of antiquities does as naturally lead to it as any other branch of knowledge whatsoever) it may be pardonable for any gentleman of the society to vary in opinion from them, on points of such very remote antiquity, as many that concern the British coins must be allowed to be: And so long as the reasons for his dissent are offered to the cognizance and arbitrament of the society with temper, moderation, and decency, no member whatsoever, nor even the parties opposed, can with any colour of reason and justice take any offence. The two gentlemen above-mentioned, I can be confident, would be the last persons disgusted in such case, as they have proposed their particular notions and sentiments with equal modesty and learning; one declaring in the words of Livy, *Quis enim rem tam veterem pro certo affirmet* (1); and the other from himself, *In re tam incertâ quisque per me suo jure utatur* (2). In respect of other authors, I need make no apology; and tho' I do not pretend to have turned into all those numerous writers, who have treated on this period of the British or Roman history, which would be almost an endless task, and serve no good purpose; yet I hope the reader will perceive the antients have not been neglected, and that recourse has been had to such of the moderns as are esteemed the best and most sensible authors; amongst whom I reckon Mr. Horseley, Mr. Carte, and the compilers of the Universal History. Those authors who have written expresly on the subject, have been in general consulted.

I shall add no more, but that the types or delineations are taken from Camden; the Earl of Pembroke's Numismata Antiqua; Dr. Pettingal's plate (from Mr. Duane's collection) prefixed to his dissertation upon the word TASCIA; the second edition of Dr. Battely's Antiq. Rutup. Oxon 1745, tab. VI. Mr. Wise, plate XVI. and Mr. Selden's Titles of honour, part I. c. viii. The true size of the coins is expressed in most of these editors, but not in Camden and Selden. As for the few coins that are not engraved, but only described, the authors of the respective descriptions are mentioned along with them.

(1) Dr. Pettingal, p. 9.
(2) Mr. Wise, p. 227.

TO

TO

THE RIGHT REVEREND

THE LORD BISHOP OF CARLISLE.

My Lord,

THAT Series of Coins, commonly called British, is attended, as to the generality of them, with the utmost difficulty and uncertainty. Some have doubted, whether they ought to be deemed coins or not; whilst others, as Mr. Wife in particular, incline to think them not the coins of this island, but to appertain to some other country (1). But your Lordship must be sensible, these coins can be of no great use, tho' they are purchased by our antiquaries at a vast expence, until it be assuredly known they belong to us, and are truly the specie of the original inhabitants of this land; nay, I presume I may go one step further, and aver, they will

(1) See his dissertation in Numm. Bodl. Catalog. p. 225. seq.

prove

prove of very trifling significance, unless we can even appropriate them, with a good degree of certainty, to the Princes who are their true and real owners; for all arguments drawn from them, relative to any disputable point of antiquity, must, till then, be extremely vague and precarious. Thus, for example, should a coin actually present us with the head of Caratacus, and another with that of Togodumnus; yet should we not know they were the coins of these Princes, we could infer nothing from them, and whilst they continued inveloped in their obscurity, they would absolutely be of no use or service to us.

What I propose therefore in the following epistle is, to ascertain the coins of Cunobelin upon some rational and at least probable principles; and herein certain incidental matters of consequence will be treated. I shall then describe and illustrate them one by one in a short commentary; which done, I may try what will be the result upon the whole in regard of our British antiquities; what light the coins may throw upon them, either directly, or by elucidating and confirming the relations of our antient authors concerning them. A laudable design, as your Lordship will easily grant, tho' difficult to execute; wherefore should I miscarry, I may yet say with Pliny the Elder, " Itaque etiam non-assecutis vo- " luisse abunde pulchrum atque magnificum est (1);" but if the principles I proceed upon should happen to be so fortunate as to approve themselves to the judgment of your Lordship, and the rest of the learned world, the candid antiquary in particular, for whose purpose this

(1) Plin. N. H. in Præf.

essay

essay is more immediately calculated, I shall think my labour well bestowed, in procuring to this suite of coins their natural use, the same as the coins of so many other nations obtain, and investing them with a rank and dignity by no means contemptible, tho' so little apprehended before; for, if I mistake not, my Lord, this series will prove a noble, comprehensive, and even interesting collection. The number of Cunobelin's coins, according to the notions I shall advance in this letter, is already great, the pieces here delineated and described being near upon forty, and in process of time will probably be much greater, when new coins are discovered; and those now latent in the cabinets of the curious are more generally brought to light. Gentlemen, in the present dark state and condition of the British cabinet, have but small encouragement to do this; but hereafter it is to be hoped, when some glimpse of day-light begins to appear, they will be induced to open and communicate their treasures. Certainly, it were much to be wished, that these coins were either all in one hand, or could be all brought together, for the sake of better comparing them; for, to apply the words of Horace,

—— " Servit collecta pecunia." ——
1 Epist. x. 47.

And should I say, that if the coins adduced by our first antiquaries Speed and Camden, were re-inspected with the same accuracy and care, which your Lordship's friend, Mr. Borlase, has used in viewing and reporting those he
has

has given us from Karn-Brê (1); no inconsiderable advantage would arise from thence, I dare say I should be justified by the event.

But here, my Lord, I must go so far out of my way as to observe, that tho' I am persuaded the coins of Cunobelin may upon rational grounds be ascertained, and very material uses may consequently be made of them, yet I have a very different opinion of the rest of this tribe; it being absolutely impossible, at this distance of time, and in that uncertainty under which we labour, both as to their nation and their personal owners, to bring them to account, or to draw any valuable advantages from them. The far greatest part of them affords us not one single letter, and, in a general way of speaking, where there is an initial syllable or two, there is no knowing, in this remote age, how to complete the word; nor whether it be the name of a prince or a mintmaster, of a nation or a town. Insomuch, that it is to be feared this numerous body of Celtic remains, to use that comprehensive term, will continue in their obscurity to the end of the world; for tho' antiquaries should write about them and about them, their dissonant and ill-grounded opinions would only serve to aggravate that perplexity, with which we are but too much embarrassed already.

As for Cunobelin, in whose time it is supposed our Saviour Christ was born, he was an illustrious British prince, made so partly by these copious, lasting, and even elegant remains, and partly by being the father of Caratacus, a more illustrious son. The antients however have delivered little more concerning him, but that he

(1) Borlase, Antiq. of Cornwal, p. 242. seq.

had two other sons, Adminius and Togodumnus (1), and was living, according to Suetonius, in Caligula's reign (2); when, for some reason, now unknown, he drove Adminius out of his kingdom, who fled into the arms of that Emperor. From hence, it should seem, he reached a good old age. It appears moreover, that he had other children besides those already mentioned, and that his seat was at Camulodunum. This is the chief of what the antients have told us in express words, and yet Alford can name the very year when he ascended the throne (3); wherefore all other particulars concerning him, his connexions with Augustus Cæsar, his intercourse with the Romans, his towns, &c. must be derived from the coins, together with certain oblique notices relative to his affairs and times, in Strabo, Tacitus, &c. which we intend shall all have a place below. Considering then, my Lord, the figure this Prince makes on the coins, and the relation he stands in to us and our native land, it may well become an antiquary to investigate every circumstance that may possibly concern him, for the elucidation of his affairs in

---

(1) Suetonius in Caligula. Dio, Lib. LX.

(2) M. Westm. p. 45, says, Kimbelin died A. D. 22, early in the reign of Tiberius, and was succeeded by Guiderius. He follows the British history in this, and is himself followed by Alford, who reckons Guiderius to be Togodumnus. Alford, in consequence of this, supposes Cunobelin to have driven his son Adminius into exile in Tiberius's time, for which, as he has no other foundation but what Matthew relates concerning the father's death, one knows not how to credit it against the authority of Suetonius. Alford pretends nobody mentions the time of Adminius's exile, but Suetonius evidently does.

(3) He reckons the 15th of Cunobelin to coincide with 1st of Christ, and 42d of Augustus, p. 3. So p. 6. he corrects Matth. Westm. for making Kimbelinus beget his sons after the 10th year of his reign, saying, it should be 19th.

particular,

particular, and the general state of the times. However, I shall endeavour to be as brief as the nature of the theme will admit; a point which I shall constantly keep in view, out of deference to those multifarious engagements which a person of your Lordship's extensive connexions must of course be involved in.

But a preliminary observation seems to be absolutely necessary here, as relating to the very existence of these coins. Bishop Nicholson has started a notion, that they were never intended for money, but were rather amulets or charms (1); and Mr. Thoresby seems to concur with him (2): but if these antient remains, for antient they doubtless are, are really not coins, but something else, 'tis in vain for us to think of proceeding any further. This matter must therefore be discussed. The Bishop's words are, " Nor does it well appear that ever afterwards " [after Julius Cæsar] their [the British] Kings brought " in any [money] of another sort. Camden says, he could " not learn that after their retirement into Wales, they " had any such thing among them, &c." But with submission, this argument is of no force against Cunobelin; since, as will be shewn, the Britons were afterwards obliged to desist from coining; by which means the art might be lost, or perhaps neglected, the Britons enjoying in the later times a sufficient quantity of the Roman specie.

The Bishop goes on to observe, ' We now have several " antient coins... which are generally reputed to be " British; though 'tis very hard to determine in what " age of the world they were minted." This, it is al-

(1) Nicholson, Hist. Libr. p. 35. edit. fol. 1714.
(2) Thoresby's Museum, p. 337.

lowed, may be true of the greatest part of these coins, but not of those where the name of Cunobelin, or some abbreviation of it, is expresly inscribed. These, methinks, we are as well assured are his, as we are, that the coins which bear the names of the Roman Emperors are theirs.

But nevertheless, the Bishop, upon these principles, rejects Mr. Camden's stories, as he calls them, *of Cunobelin, and Queen Brundvica,* saying, they are much of a piece with Dr. Plott's Prasutagus; and then he declares openly, " for my part, I am of opinion, that never any " of the British Kings did coin money: but that even " their tribute money (like the Dane-gelt and Peter- " pence afterwards) was the ordinary current coin which " was brought in (or minted here) by the Romans them- " selves, as long as this island continued a province." He then says, " He takes the most (if not all) of the fore- " mentioned pieces to be... amulets," and then quotes this passage from Tho. Bartholin, " Habuere veteres in " paganismo res quasdam portatiles, ex argento vel auro " factas, imaginibus deorum facie humanâ expressorum " signatas, quibus futurorum cognitionem explorabant, et " quarum possessione felices se et quodam quasi numinis " præsidio tutos judicabant," adding, " these were in use " among the Romans a good while after they came into " Britain," and citing Spartianus.

But what! Cunobelin's coins are not to be put on the same footing with the reputed ones of Boadicea and Prasutagus; for these may be falsly attributed to them, as I believe they are, whilst the specie pretending to be Cunobelin's may be really and truly his. It will be debated hereafter, whether the Britons paid any tribute in money,

or

or not; at present therefore I only remark, that as to the Bishop's supposition, that it might be paid in Roman money, this appears to me to be altogether impossible, since the *Vectigal* was imposed by Julius Cæsar, when there was no Roman money in the island; and when paid afterwards, in Cunobelin's and Augustus Cæsar's time for example, there is as little reason to believe there was any there then. As to the passage from Bartholin, it is entirely beside the purpose; for the author does not say the *things* he speaks of were of the nature of money: they might be images or any thing else; and, I may add, with what propriety can any one argue from the practices of the Danes, to the Britons, so long before the former had any thing to do with our island? So again the quotation from Spartian amounts to little or nothing; for all he says, is, that at Rome in Caracalla's time, *such were condemned as carried about their necks certain remedies against Quartans and Tertians.* But now the pieces here in question were very unfit to be so carried, not one of them being ever seen with a hole, or a ring, adapted to that purpose, as is usual in coins that have been worn about the neck (1). And whereas Serenus Sammonicus, a physician of note, lived in this reign, and in his book *de Medicina* has described certain medicines and charms to be worn about the neck, for the curing of the Tertian and the *Hemitritæum*, and particularly the *Abrasadabra* for a remedy against the latter, most people will think the remedies spoken of by Spartian were of that kind, were of the nature of Abraxas, or Abrasadabra, concerning

(1) Lord Pembroke, Part III. Tab. 109.

which

which see Montfaucon (1) and Fabricius (2); however, nobody will imagine they were at all like cups or amulets. Wherefore, to summ up all in a word, as these pieces have all the appearances of coin that can be desired, with an obverse and reverse, I can see no reason why we should not deem them such. The name of Cunobelin written at length on some of them, clearly shews they can be no amulets, but must be money. The same may be said concerning the initials of that name. Besides, how should such quantities of these pieces be found together, as at Karn-Brê, upon the supposition of their being amulets (3)? To which I shall only add, how strange it is, Cunobelin and his Britons should imitate the Romans in the use of amulets alone, and not in their coins, which seems so much more natural and obvious? To speak plainly, my Lord, your Lordship's learned predecessor at Carlisle has not acquitted himself with his usual judgment and penetration on the present occasion, but rather loosely and superficially, to say no worse.

All I shall note further in a general way, is, that most of these coins are disk'd, more or less, with a concave and a convex side; that they are of various metals, gold, silver, brass, but often extremely debased; and that an eminent antiquary has been so exact as to give us the weight of many of them (4). But little, I doubt, can be discovered from thence, the data concerning such matters in these times being but few or none.

(1) Montf. II. p. 240.
(2) Fabricius, Bibl. Lat. I. p. 541. III. p. 81.
(3) Borlase, Antiq. of Cornwall, p. 242.
(4) Borlase, Antiq. of Cornwall.

To enter now on the subject. The coins published and described by our authors, that can with any degree of certainty be thought the money of Cunobelin (1), are here brought together, for the sake of affording us an advantageous view of them; and they may be commodiously distributed into the following arrangement:

I. Those that present us with the King's name only, or some abbreviation of it.

II. Such as bear his name with a place of coinage.

III. Such as afford us his name along with TASCIA, or some abbreviation of that word.

IV. Those that exhibit the King's name along with TASCIA, and a place of coinage also.

V. Those that have TASCIA only.

VI. Those that give us TASCIA with a place of coinage.

This distribution, 'tis presumed, will be just, and, we hope, useful, let what will be the sense and meaning of the word TASCIA or TASCIO; it will probably serve for all coins of this King, that yet may lie hidden in the cabinets of the curious. For my own part, to come closer to the point, I esteem them all to be the coins of our famous Cunobelin, and I shall here endeavour to assure

(1) Coins are sometimes conjectured to belong to this Prince, that have no medium in the word to connect them with him; as that in Thoresby, p. 338.

them to him by certain arguments and observations; as also by removing such difficulties and objections as may have been raised against his claim.

As to the first and second class, a very shrewd remark has fallen from the pen of a very sagacious and learned author: Mr. Wise acknowledges, that where we find CVNOBELIN or CVNOB, it may be the name of a person; but if there be only CVN or CVNO he is doubtful about it, since these may be the initials of some other word, of the name of a people or city for example. Something of the same kind was dropped formerly by Mr. Walker, " per- " haps, said he, CVNO, signifying (as Camden observes) a " Prince, may be applied (especially since many coins " have no more than CVNO) to divers Princes, as it is ad- " ded to the end of the names of several, mentioned in " Gildas (1)." Mr. Wise observes further, that he does not remember ever to have seen CAM or CAMV on the same coin with CVNOB, but only with CVN or CVNO, for which reason he does not affirm there was any connexion between CAMV and CVNOBELIN; and why, says he, on the contrary, may not CAMV be the name of a man, and CVNO the name of a people or city? *Camulus* is the name of a deity worshiped by the *Etrurians*, and perhaps by the *Celtæ*. He imagines that coin in Speed's hist. p. 31 (2). with the letters CAMV, and on the reverse CVNO, may exhibit the head of this deity. Afterwards it might become a regal name. In like manner by CVN, the *Cunei*, a people of *Spain*, who are called by *Ptolemy Bœtici Celtici*, may be intended, or *Cuniſtorgis*, a city of theirs, or the

(1) Walker in Camden, col. CXV.
(2) Camden I. No. 21.

Taru

Taru Cunomienses of *Gallia Narbonensis*, for Pere *Harduin* in his notes on *Pliny*, Lib. III. seems to have rejected the first syllables *Taru*. Mr. Wise afterwards, p. 227. mentions the city *Cunetio*. He concludes, " Seu ergo Cuno-
" belin Tascio Cunobelinum Tascodunorum, seu Britan-
" niæ, regem interpretari velint eruditi, non multum
" moror; in re tam incertâ quisque per me suo jure
" utatur (1)."

These remarks are weighty, and intitled doubtless to a serious consideration; and yet, I think, a satisfactory answer may be given to them all. First, it appears from the third and fourth class above, that Cunobelin had a connexion with Tascio, whatever sense we put upon that word, for on some of them his name occurs, written at full length along with Tascio; wherefore is it not more than probable, for we pretend not to demonstration, that such pieces as exhibit only CVN and CVNO with TASCIO must be his; and that these are plainly abbreviations of his name? Certainly, they ought not, by any rule of interpretation, to be taken for any thing else, for the name of a city or people, for instance, as this gentleman conjectures. The argument, my Lord, runs thus: Cunobelin is connected with Tascio, and Cuno is connected also therewith, therefore Cunobelin and Cuno must be the same person.

By parity of reason, if coins with CVN or CVNO, when found in conjunction with TASCIO, be Cunobelin's, the other pieces, with CVN or CVNO alone, should be his, tho' TASCIO does not appear. The case here seems to be equally plain; for if CVN or CVNO, in one instance, be the abbre-

(1) Wise, Catal. p. 226.

viation

viation of Cunobelin, it ought to be esteemed so in another, provided there be no particular reason to the contrary, as there is not here. Those coins again which present us with CVN or CVNO, and VER or CAMV, or some other word, must be deemed to be Cunobelin's, tho' TASCIO does not appear upon them; especially, if an interpretation can be put upon these initials, consistent with the affairs of Cunobelin, as may be done in this case. Now VER, we think, may stand very naturally for Verulam, and CAMV for Camulodunum, both of them known to be towns or cities within the precincts of this Prince's dominions; and HICV, we judge, must be a name of the same kind, tho' it be not so easy at this day to determine what place that was. As to Camulodunum, Dio expressly calls it the palace or principal seat of Cunobelin (1); and we know it was soon after made a Roman colony, and the first in Britain, a circumstance very favourable to the appearance of its name upon the coins. Camulodunum seems to take its name from the warlike deity, Camulus (2), worshiped in a peculiar and extraordinary manner there, as might well be expected from a prince of so martial a disposition as Cunobelin will be shewn to be. Mr. Baxter, I know, gives us a different etymology of the name, from *Cam a laün üi dun* (3);

and

(2) Camden, col. 416. Montf. VI. p. 53. Alford, p. 6.

(1) Μάχη τε ἵκησι καὶ τὸ Καμυλόδουνον τὸ τὸ Κυνοβελίνα βασίλειον ἦν. Dio, p. 781. speaking of Claudius.

(3) " Etymon hujus urbis planè Britannicum est; nam si solutè scribatur,
" *Cam a laün üi dun, Civitas* erit *ad Alauni* sive *Pleni amnis curvaturam.* At-
" que hoc confirmant cognomina loci, et *Camalan* in Ottadinniis, et *Co-*
" *malan* apud Damnios in Valentia. Atque hinc quidem constat fluvium ho-
" die

and Mr. Sammes thinks it comes from *Camol*, which in the Phœnician language fignifies *a prince or governor*, and the old *Dun* a hill; fo that Camulodunum may be called the King's hill, as Mons Capitolinus at Rome fignified Jupiter's hill. But certainly, the above etymon appears fo eafy and natural, that one cannot but prefer it to Mr. Baxter's; and as to Sammes, Bifhop Gibfon writes; "How it will fuit with the old altar infcription, which "mentions CAMULVS DEVS, and with the coins which con- "firm it, I much doubt; and yet thofe muft be looked "upon as the beft authorities;" by which it is plain his Lordfhip is in our party, as in reafon he may, fince it is fcarcely credible the Phœnicians fhould ever have had any thing to do with that part of the ifland where Camulodunum lay. But to return: It is infinuated that CAMV may poffibly be the initial fyllables, not of Camulodunum, but of fomething elfe, perhaps the name of a man, as CVNO may be the name of a people or city; and the allegation in fupport of this notion is, that Camulus is the name of a deity, worfhiped by the Etrurians, and perhaps by the Celtæ. We admit every thing in regard to the god Camulus, but cannot avoid remarking, that the fuggeftion from thence is but barely poffible; and moreover, that as we have cleared the matter fufficiently in refpect of CVN and CVNO, we have now all the reafon in the world to expound CAMV, in fome fenfe that may be confiftent therewith; in a word, to take it for the

"die dictum de loco *Coloniam*, olim fuiffe *Alaunum*. Spectabat hæc urbs ad "Trinoüantes Ptolemæi ævo; cum olim fedes fuerit Cunobelini Icenorum "Imperatoris." Baxter, Gloff. in v.
(1) Camd. col. CIX. and 351.

COINS OF CUNOBELIN. 15

name of a place, and in particular of Camulodunum. Mr. Wife imagines the coin in Speed, with the letters CAMV, and on the reverfe CVNO, may exhibit the head of the god Camulus. But now allowing that Camulus might be a deity of the Britons in particular, as well as of the Etrurians and the Celtæ, it will by no means follow that the head in Speed reprefents him; on the contrary, it may feem demonftrably plain it does not, becaufe this word CAMV is written along with an ear of corn in claff. II. no. 2. and 4. under an animal, a Hog, I fuppofe (1), in claff. II. no. 1. and under a Pegafus in Lord Pembroke, claff. II. no. 6. This laft is the more remarkable, becaufe this imaginary being, the flying horfe, is feen on a coin, with TASCE infcribed underneath, and which gives us on the other fide CAMV, within a laureate crown, claff. III. no. 2. The prefumption therefore is, that the head on the coin in queftion reprefents fome other perfon, and not the god Camulus; that moft probably it is the refemblance of Cunobelin himfelf, the abbreviation of whofe name appears on all thefe feveral coins.

To fpeak a word more in this place of this deity. The God of war feems to have had different names in various parts of the ifland; amongft the Trinobantes or Cattuvellauni, to have been called Camulus; by the Brigantes, Belatucadrus; by the Coritani, Braciaca; and perhaps by others, Hefus or Efus (2). Mr. Sammes, Mr. Selden,

(1) Compare Lord Pembroke, P. II. plate 94.
(2) Lucan L 445. Lact. L. 21. Montf. II. p. 266, 270.

Mr.

Mr. Hearne and Montfaucon (1), all take Belatucadrus to be the fame as Belenus of the Gauls, or Apollo; but Mr. Baxter, who gives us the etymology of this barbarous word, efteems him with more reafon to be the fame as Mars; and it is evident from an infcription in Horfley and Gale, that he was fo.

DEO MARTI
BELATVCADRO, &c. (2).

Hence Richard of Cirencefter writes, p. 9. " Hinc Apollinem, Martem, qui etiam Vitucadrus appellabatur (3). Dr. Gale alfo, tho' at firft he was of opinion Belatucadrus was the name of a river (4); yet afterwards feems to hint from this very infcription, that he might be Mars, and prefents us with an etymology agreeable thereunto (5). Mr. Hearne, for his part, was aware of this explanatory infcription, and therefore pretends that Apollo Sagittarius, for the affiftance he is fuppofed to have given in military affairs, is therein ftiled Mars Belatucadrus. But if the plaineft and moft exprefs monuments are to be explained away in this manner, they will prove of very little fervice to us; and I would fubmit it to your Lordfhip's decifion, whether it be not infinitely more natural, and more con-

(1) Selden, de diis Syris. Synt. II. c. 1. Hearne, in Lel. Itin. I. p. 137. VIII. p. xviii. Montf. II. p. 268.
(2) Horfeley, p. 271. and Gale's Antoninus, p. 34.
(3) Certain places in the ifland, as appears from Richard, were named from Hercules; but thefe, we prefume, were in the poft-Roman times.
(4) Gale, Comment. in Antonin. p. 33.
(5) " Agnofco tamen alteram nuper Æficre detectam Belatucadrum " Martemque velut deum colere cundem, pofteriorque pars dictionis ali- " quid fpirat iftius numinis; cum *Cad* prælium, *Cader* caftrum, & *Cadr* " fortis Britannice fonent, quæ omnia Marti fatis congruunt". Ibid. p. 34.

siftent with reason and common sense, that Belatucadrus should here be an attribute or synonyme of Mars, rather than that, on the contrary, Mars should be an epithet of his; and indeed, according to this acceptation, Braciaca will be called Mars (and not Mars, Braciaca) in the inscription which I am now going to adduce, and consequently, be a different deity from Mars, which yet nobody, I believe, will ever admit.

As to this Braciaca, the Romans had doubtless great concerns with the Peak of Derbyshire; and in the grounds belonging to Haddon house.... was dug up this altar, cut in a rough fort of stone, such as the house itself is built of.

<pre>
        DEO
       MARTI
     BRACIACAE
      OSITTIVS
     CAECILIAN
     PRAEFECT
      TRO....
       VS. (1)
</pre>

This altar could not be found when Mr. Horsley enquired for it; however, the above inscription was copied by Mr. Stonehouse, Rector of Darfield, Com. Ebor. whose collection of antiquities at length came into the hands of Mr. Ralph Thoresby of Leeds (2); and

---

(1) Camden, col. 592. The stone is the greet stone of the country; but the house is not built of that, to speak of the whole of it, but of limestone.

(2) Bishop Gibson says, " They were purchased by Mr. Thoresby of " Leeds," meaning Mr. John Thoresby. The exact truth is, that, on the death of Mr. Walter Stonehouse, who was a great sufferer in the grand rebellion,

and this inscription, I presume, was communicated to Bishop Gibson by that gentleman. There were one or two more inscriptions, which were broken and very imperfect, and without any direction, in Mr. Stonehouse's papers, where they were found, insomuch, that it is uncertain whether at Haddon or not. As to the inscription before us, Mr. Horsley inclines to think Haddon might be called Braciaca in the Roman times (1); but I rather think it an epithet or local name of the God of war, like to Belatucadrus; and this I find is the opinion of Mr. Baxter, who writes, " Braciaca in Camdeni (2) in-
" scriptione *Mars* est; quasi dicas hodiernâ Britannorum
" scripturâ *Braichiaüc*, sive *Brachiosus*, & per hoc *præ-*
" *validus*. Formâ hic erat forsanganteâ, cum *Brachiis*
" plurimis, quod in medio relinquimus." He supposes the word *Braciaca* may be formed of the British *Brachi-aüc*, from *Braich*, an arm, and so signify *Brachiosus*, that is, *prævalidus*; and thereupon conjectures, which is doubtless very ingenious, that the image of the deity might be a colossus, with a large number of arms. But be this as it will, I saw this altar at Haddon, where it stands under cover in the passage leading to the chapel, A. D. 1761, in company with some gentlemen of Bakewell; but the letters are now in a state of evanescence, and we could but just make them out.

To return back to our subject: The connexion between Cunobelin and Camu appears, we think, most clearly, by

bellion, being both displaced from his living and imprisoned, they were bought by Thomas Lord Fairfax; after whose decease, Mr. John Thoresby bought them as part of that Lord's collection.

(1) Horsley, p. 318. and his map..
(2) Rather Bishop Gibson's insertion in Camden.

the

the medium of TASCIA occurring with both. See the third and the sixth class. And whereas it is noted, that by CVN may be meant the Cunei, a people of Spain, or Cuniftorgis, a city of theirs, or the Cunonienfes, a nation of Gallia Narbonenfis; one has no reason to think so much old Spanish money, or specie of Narbonne, as is marked with the letters CVN and CVNO, would be found here, or that the coin of those countries was so neat and elegant as these pieces are. This conjecture is certainly too far fetched; and I shall here transcribe the words of Mr. Borlafe, as containing an argument of weight and consequence in respect of the true proprietors both of these, and others pretending and claiming to be real British coins.

" Now, says Mr. Borlafe, all these coins from Camden
" and Speed, are found in Britain in several places, many
" in number, and the very same in no other country.
" Their inscriptions, and several others which might be
" here mentioned, have either the first, or more syllables
" of British princes (1), cities, or people, nay, CVNOBELIN
" the whole name; why then should they not be Bri-
" tish? If there be honey enough in our own hive, what
" need have we to fly abroad, and range into the names
" of neighbouring countries and kings to find out refem-
" blances in found, which are not near so exact as what
" we find at home? Before we deprive our own country
" of the honour of coining the money found here, one
" would think it but reasonable that there should be pro-
" duced from foreign countries, samples of the very coins

(1) Here, I doubt, this excellent author is wrong; but, however, it does not affect the argument.

"we find in Britain, and in greater number, as being
"doubtlefs more plenty where they were ftruck, than
"any where elfe; but there is not one inftance of coins
"found abroad, which are of the fame kind as what we
"find here; altho' in Roman coins (which were not
"coined by little particular ftates, as the Britifh muft
"have been) nothing is more common. It is very won-
"derful that all the Gaulifh coins (for inftance) corre-
"fpondent to ours in metal and workmanfhip, fhould be
"deftroyed, and not one appear or be dug up in Gaul,
"whereas in Britain they are numerous, which makes the
"learned Mr. Wife (1), though dubious at other times,
"conclude very juftly, that no country has a better title
"to the coining them than Britain (2)." In brief, my
Lord, there is no room for the above furmifes of Mr. Wife,
fince CVN and CVNO are fo evidently connected with
TASCIO in the third and fourth claffes, a term which appears only upon the coins found in this ifland, and, I fuppofe, I may add, on thofe of Cunobelin only.

But is it not ftrange, your Lordfhip will fay, no coins of
Togodumnus, Caratacus, Adminius, or other Britifh
princes, fhould be found, but only coins of Cunobelin (3)?
I anfwer, there is nothing very extraordinary in this, all
circumftances confidered. It appears from Suetonius,
that Cunobelin was living in Caligula's time (4), and
early in the next reign Britain was invaded by the Romans, after which, as it fhould feem, the Britons were

(1) " Maximo fane numero in hac infula eruuntur, adeo ut nulla regio
poffeffionis jure magis eos (viz. nummos) fibi vendicet ?" Wife, p. 228.
(2) Mr. Borlafe, p. 252. and again, p. 258.
(3) Wife, p. 226. Walker, in Camd. col. CXV.
(4) Sueton. in Caio, c. 44.

not

COINS OF CUNOBELIN.

not permitted to coin any more money; obferve the words of Gildas, "Non Britannia, fed Romana infula cenferetur, et quicquid habere potuiffet æris, argenti, vel auri, imagine Cæfaris notaretur (1):" a paffage that plainly excludes the pretended coins of Prafutagus, Boadicea, Arviragus, &c. and even of Togodumnus, Caratacus, and Adminius, the immediate fucceffors of Cunobelin.

I proceed now on the third and fourth claffes, where I apprehend I fhall have much to fay, thefe claffes being of the moft importance, as fhewing the connexion of Cunobelin with TASCIO, the medium of appropriation, whatever is the meaning of the word, and as being particularly fubfervient to the allotment of the fifth and fixth fort to this Prince.

But here arifes a grand queftion, What is the fenfe and meaning of this word TASCIO, fo varioufly written, and with fo many abbreviations? There are two different opinions concerning this word propofed already. Thefe, my Lord, I fhall difcufs; and afterwards fhall offer another of my own.

The firft and moft antient interpretation is that of Mr. Camden and Dr. Powel (2), which has fince been efpoufed by many other writers (3), and of late has been fupported with great learning by Dr. Pettingal (4). Mr.

(1) Gildas, p. 3.
(2) Camd. col. CIX. and 351.
(3) Baxter, Gloff. in v. et v. CUNOBELINUS, ARVIRAGUS. Thorefby in Mufeo, p. 338. Univ. Hift. XIX. p. 130. Carte, p. 98. Alford, p. 4. Horfley, p. 15. W. Vallans, in Lel. Itin. V. p. XV.
(4) Differt. on the TASCIA, or Legend on the Britifh coins of Cunobelin and others, printed by the Society of Antiquaries, Lond. 4to. 1763.

Camden's

Camden's words are, that on the reverse of the second of Cunobelin's coins in his plate is, " The mint-master, with " the addition of the word TASCIA; which in British sig- " nifies a tribute penny (as I am informed by David Powel, " a person admirably skilled in that language) so called, " perhaps, from the Latin *Taxatio*; for the Britons do not " use the letter x. And on the same account, we often " see MONETA upon the Roman coins."

Dr. Pettingal's first proposition is, that the vectigal imposed by Julius Cæsar upon the Britons, at the close of his second expedition to this island, " was called TASCIA in " the British language of the country, from *Tag*, the " prince, chief, that collected and paid it to the Romans." The sum and substance of his Dissertation he afterwards gives us in these words, " The meer English word *Tax*, " is perhaps a corruption of *Task*.—*Task* is derived from " *Tascia* of the antient Britons, and *Tascia* was the " *vectigal* or tribute, paid by the *Tag* or British Prince " of each province, to the Roman conquerors (1);" whereupon it is necessary to observe, that as he calls it a tribute in this passage, so he elsewhere supposes it to be a pecuniary payment (2), and to be paid in a species of money coined for that particular purpose (3); and these indeed are the sentiments of most of the other gentlemen cited above.

But now to canvass these principles and positions, and to bring them to the test of reason; does it not appear extremely forced and unnatural to those who are not Bri-

(1) Pettingal, p. 9.
(2) Dissert. p. 5. and see Alford, p. 2.
(3) Ibid.

tons, and have but little skill in that language, that *Tascia* should grow, as Dr. Pettingal supposes, from *Tag*? Doubtless, a question may very properly and very innocently be asked, whether this deviation be according to the usual analogy of the British language? In short, my Lord, it does not seem sufficient in this case, to prove to us that the Celtic *Tag* signified a name of eminence among the Britons, which the Doctor, it must be acknowledged, has very satisfactorily done, since we want to be further convinced that *Tascia* is regularly and idiomatically deduced from it. Certainly the process of this extraordinary derivation ought to have been well illustrated and fully established, since so much depends upon it, and it seems justly doubtful to an English ear.

But supposing for once, that the word *Tascia* is canonically, and, according to the idiom of the antient British language, deducible from the word *Tag*, and that the British chief or Prince collected the tribute, as the Doctor advances; yet I doubt it will not follow, that the word TASCIA on the coins of Cunobelin must signify *Tribute*. In this consists a wide difference betwixt the Doctor's notions and mine. 'Tis contrary, in my opinion, to usage and the nature of things, for a species of money to be struck meerly for the purpose of paying tribute; and there lies a strong objection against this interpretation of the word Tascia, upon that account. 'Tis true this sense of the word is espoused by great names (1), as has been noted; but it is nevertheless clogged, when it comes to be maturely considered, with many, and perhaps unsurmountable difficulties. The money advanced by the Jews for

(1) Wise, p. 226.

the

the maintenance and support of the service of the temple, was the current coin of the country, and not purposely stamp'd (1); and the tribute-money paid by that people to the Romans, after they were become a province, was the Roman coin current in Judæa (2), insomuch that, without alledging any other instances, one may reasonably demand an authority, or example of a species of money coined solely for the purpose of its being paid in tribute, in any nation. It was fancied, I know, formerly, that those Anglo-Saxon pennies, styled Peterpence, were struck for the making of the payment that was called by that name; but gentlemen are now convinced, that they are only Saxon pennies coined at York, and that the Peter-pence was always paid in the current specie; as also was the Danegeld; and indubitably and universally, the common way of paying tribute, whenever it is done in money, is to discharge it in the current coin of the country, and not in a particular sort struck for that sole end and purpose. But possibly it may be replied, that if the Britons had no money current amongst them, but the first coinage was in consequence of the *vectigal* imposed by Julius Cæsar, their case was particular, and money might be fabricated for the purpose of paying tribute here, tho' proceedings were different in other states. This objection will be considered below, where we shall have occasion to specify the nature of this *vectigal*, as likewise when, and by what means, the Britons first stamped money; and then it will be shewn, that the

(1) Matth. xvii. 24. seq.
(2) Matth. xxii. 17. seq.

specie

specie first coined in Britain was probably for general use. At present I shall go on.

As the foregoing remark, that no nation ever struck money for the meer purpose of paying it in tribute, seems to be of weight, does it not effectually preclude all endeavours of fixing a sense of *tribute* upon the word in question? and consequently to explode that wild and groundless notion of Mr. Camden, " That, for the tribute " payable by the Britons, coins were stamp'd for the " greater cattle with a horse, for lesser with a hog, for " woods with a tree, and for corn-ground with an ear of " corn?" Mr. Wise very justly taxes him for this. Nor does that conception of Cardinal Baronius appear to be better founded, that the tribute money differ'd from the common money, and was altered according to the different quality of the tribute, when the common money continued the same as before (1). These surely are strange fancies, unworthy of the great authors concerned, and contrary to all usual methods of proceeding.

The observation of the learned Mr. Wise, who is not more favourable to our antiquaries in their interpretation of the word Tascia, than myself, seems to be of great moment. He asks, where it was ever known, that money, every where esteemed a mark of royalty and freedom, was stamp'd with such a note of servitude upon it, as the word TASCIO implies, according to the sense they give it? Mr. Camden indeed remarks, that we often see MONETA on the Roman coins, and it is confessed we do; but in those cases MONETA is an honourable word, as well it might be, since she was enshrined by the name of DEA

(1) Baronius in Camden, col. CXIII. See his opinion confuted by Casaubon, Exerc. xvi. n. 10.

PECVNIA, in the figure of a woman holding a pair of ballances in one hand, and a cornucopia in another (1)? But how ill does this comport with Tafcio, in Mr. Camden's fenfe of this term; according to which, it betokens nothing but ignominy and difgrace? Certainly, there is fomething exceffively fervile, incongruous, and even abfurd, in putting a word of fuch a bafe import upon the Britifh coins, as this people had not been in fact reduced to an abject ftate; on the contrary, were but in a fmall part, and that part very imperfectly fubdued: nay, I may foreftal what I fhall prove hereafter, fo far as to fay, that the Britons, inftead of being enflaved in Cunobelin's time by the Romans, lived in great harmony and friendfhip with them.

Conclufive as thefe obfervations may feem to be, I would add, by way of fupporting them further, if thought needful, that many of thefe coins are of brafs or copper; whereupon Alford obferves, " Romanorum tamen cenfus " erat elegantior, nec ære, aut ferro folvendus." But what is more decifive, brafs was not native then in Britain, we being exprefly told by Cæfar, concerning the Britons, *ære utuntur importato* (2). But now, my Lord, who would not fuppofe, if money was to be coined with the fpecial view of paying tribute, that it would be in fome metal of the country; tin, or lead, or iron? Indeed, one cannot imagine how a country fo little engaged in commerce, as this ifland, more efpecially the Eaftern part of it, then was, could have any large quantity of a foreign metal in it. In the Weft, where the tin was, and perhaps lead, I prefume there might be more

(1) Camd. Remains, p. 178.
(2) Cæf. de B. G. l. V. c. 12.

traffic with foreigners; but in the Eastern, or South-Eastern parts, they had only some little trade with the opposite continent of Gaul. Besides, the Romans did not want brass, tho' the Britons did; but supposing the Romans had occasion for it, what the Britons could pay them this way must have been very inconsiderable, since others of the coins with TASCIA, or some abbreviation of it upon them, are silver, and others gold. But had the Romans wanted this metal, bullion, or copper in the mass, would have served their purpose just as well, or perhaps better than coined money; for I much question whether, if the tribute had been paid in money, such money would have passed abroad; in Gaul or Italy, for example. We have no reason to think the brass money of the Seleucidæ, or of the Grecian states, ever passed current at Rome: the silver and gold indeed of the Eastern parts might have a currency there, as having a considerable intrinsic value; but the case was very different with copper or brass. Upon the whole, my Lord, the tribute, upon this hypothesis, seems to have been of a very aukward kind, since it must have proved of so little use to the receivers, whether kept in the form of coin, or melted down.

But as to the fact of this pecuniary payment, Julius Cæsar on his first expedition demanded nothing but hostages (1), which the Britons being negligent in sending, this afforded him a pretence for his second invasion. At the end of this latter attempt, wherein he had been more successful, and had penetrated further into the country, he imposed a yearly payment, amongst other articles,

(1) Cæf. de B. G. l. IV. 27, 31, 36, 38.

upon the Britons, in the shape and under the name of a *Vectigal*, " Et quid in annos singulos *Vectigalis* Populo " R. Britannia penderet, constituit (1)." But now, my Lord, *Vectigal* does not necessarily imply a payment in money, as the writers on the subject will inform you (2); and tho' the words *Tributum* and *Vectigal* may be now and then confounded in less accurate authors (3); and later writers, when they speak of this transaction, will call the impost in question a tribute (4), and will even go so far as to specify the exact summ that was paid, viz. 3000*l*. in silver (5); yet Cæsar was too great a master of the Roman language to use *Vectigal* for a pecuniary payment. Besides, if the Britons had no coined money amongst them at this time, as in all probability they had not (6), specie or coin could not possibly be any part of this annual payment. The Vectigal consequently to be paid by the Britons to the Romans, in consequence of this imposition, consisted of commodities of some kind or other; and in certain proportions of them, the aborigines of our island, at that juncture, being much in the same case with the natives of North-America at this day, who, were they to make any yearly payment to the English, would in all probability discharge it in Furs.

(1) Ibid. l. V. 22.
(2) Lipsius, de Magn. Rom. lib. II. c. 2. Bulengerus in Græv. Thes. T. VIII. P. Buman. de Vectigal, P. R. p. 2.
(3) Burman, ibid.
(4) Matth. Westm. p. 45. Alford, p. 1, 2. Univ. History XIX. p. 128, 129.
(5) Jeffr. Monm. IV. 10. MS. Chronicle, penes me. Fabian fol. XVIII. Alford, p. 2.
(6) See below.

This

COINS OF CUNOBELIN. 29

This Vectigal seems to have been converted afterwards into a duty upon exports and imports, paid in the ports of Gaul (1), which were the *Emporia*; Strabo telling us, concerning the Britons, τέλη τε ἅπως ὑπομένουσι ἐλαφέα, τῶν τε ἐξαγομένων εἰς τὴν Κελτικὴν ἐκεῖθεν καὶ τῶν εἰσαγομένων ἐνθένδε· *That the Romans laid no heavy imposts upon them, neither on the articles exported from Britain into Gaul, nor on those imported from thence* (2). This custom or duty was totally different from a tribute, and he expressly distinguishes it therefrom, for he goes on, ὥςε μηδὲν δεῖν φρουρᾶς τῆς νήσου· τἐλάχιςον μὲν γὰρ, ἑνὸς τάγματος χρήζοι ἄν, ἢ ἱππικῦ τινος, ὥςε ἢ φόρους ἀπάγεσθαι παρ' αὐτῶν· εἰς ἴσον δὴ καθίςατο πᾶν τὸ ἀνάλωμα τῇ ςραλιᾷ τοῖς προσφερομένοις χρήμασιν· ἀνάγκη γὰρ μειῦσθαι τὰ τέλη φόρων ἐπιβαλλομένων· ἅμα δὲ καὶ κινδύνες ἀπαντᾶν τινας, βίας ἐπαγομένης. *Insomuch, that there was no occasion for a garrison in the island. For one legion at least, and a body of horse, would be requisite, if tribute was to be levied there; and the expence of maintaining a garrison would run away with the whole of our receipts from thence; for the Vectigalia would necessarily be lessened, were the Britons to pay tribute; and if we were to use force in levying it, some danger might arise from thence.* Strabo writes much to the same purpose in another place, where he assigns this for the reason why the Romans in his time did not trouble themselves about making a conquest of Britain, πλέον γὰρ ἂν ἐκ τῶν τελῶν δοκεῖ προσφέρεσθαι νῦν, ἢ ὁ φόρος δύναται συντελεῖν, ἀφαιρεμέ-

(1) Mr. Carte thinks the Romans had Publicans resident here. See him, p. 97. and 98; but quære, since there seems to be no better authority for this than Gildas, p. 3.
(2) Strabo, lib. IV. p. 200.

νης τῆς εἰς τὸ ϛρατιωτικὸν δαπάνης, τὸ φευρῆσον κ̣ φορολογῆσον τὴν νῆσον· *For the Romans receive more now from the customs, than the tribute would amount to, deducting the charges of maintaining a military force to keep the island, and to collect the tribute* (1). And I think it highly probable, that at this time the *Portoria*, or customs upon exports and imports, were paid the same way, viz. by some share or proportion of the commodities. But now, if this was the case, TASCIO or TASCIA, on the coins of Cunobelin, cannot in reason be thought to have any connexion with tribute or tribute-money, as the learned gentlemen above-mentioned have interpreted it. Mr. Baxter indeed says, after Mr. Camden, " Cudebantur sane primi " Romanorum (I suppose he means here in Britain; but " quære, if it be not a mistake of Romanorum for Britan- " norum) nummi quo portoria solverentur (2)". But this is not at all likely, for the reasons above-given: he adds, " Et monetarii erant Romani", an assertion which I believe to be true, as will be shewn hereafter, but entirely inconsistent with his position, that the money first struck in Britain was for the payment of the *portoria*, since the vectigalia and the portoria were probably paid before, and in another way.

Your Lordship, on this occasion, will doubtless recollect, that, about the time of the nativity of our Saviour, Augustus Cæsar caused all the world to be taxed (3); but by this we are only to understand all the provinces of the Roman Empire, of which Britain was by no means in

(1) Strabo, lib. II. p. 116.
(2) Baxter, Gloss. v. TASCIA.
(3) Luke ii. 1.

the number; wherefore, when Nennius says, "In tem-
"pore illius [Claudii] quievit dari censum Romanis a
"Britannia, sed Britannicis imperatoribus redditum est 1),"
one hardly knows what to make of it. Certainly, if any
regard be had to what has been so lately alledged from
Strabo, one would think tribute had rather begun to be
paid, than ceased, in this Emperor's reign, whom Nennius, in the same place, calls the conqueror of Britain (2),
and says, he even subjugated the Orcades, and made them
tributary: nay, 'tis clear from Tacitus, that from this
date the Britons actually did pay tribute, "Ipsi Britanni,
"says he, delectum, *ac tributa,* & injuncta imperii mu-
"nera impigre obeunt, si injuriæ absint (3)". And
Galgacus, speaking to his troops, says of the Romans,
"Bona fortunasque in tributum egerunt; in annonam
"frumentum (4);" wherefore I cannot help thinking,
that if the MSS. would countenance (but I do not find
any various reading) we ought to read *affluxit* in Nennius, or some such word, instead of *quievit*; whereby the
sense would be, that in the reign of Claudius, tribute began to be paid by this island to the Romans, being paid
to their Generals that commanded here, meaning Aulus
Plautius and his successors.

These, my Lord, are the reasons that induce me to
conclude, in respect of the common notion concerning
the word TASCIA, on the coins of Cunobelin, that it cannot be the true one; or in other words, that these coins

(1) Nennius, c. 17.
(2) So also Pomp. Mela, III. 6.
(3) Tacit. Vit. Agric. c. 13.
(4) Ibid. c. 31.

were

were not struck meerly for the purpose of being paid in tribute to the Romans. On the contrary, as the Roman money was not current in Britain in any quantity, nor the island fully subdued, at this time, Cunobelin, and the other British Princes, I am of opinion, coined money in their own right, for their own and the common use of their subjects; and the coins in question I esteem to be of that sort. 'Tis doubted indeed, by Mr. Wise, whether the petty Kings of Britain put their effigies upon their money (1); and in truth, we have no certain evidence of any but Cunobelin that did so; but class. I. 1. II. 1. IV. 1, 2, 3, all of them Camdenian coins, present us with the head of this Prince very evidently. There is a doubt also started about the right allowed by the Romans to the nations they had conquered (2); but this does not reach the money of Cunobelin (3), who never was so totally subjected by the Roman arms, as to be reduced to the state of a provincial vassal (4), but only seems to have consented, for the sake of peace and quietness, to pay the vectigal or portorium (5).

I come now in the next place to Mr. Wise's opinion: This gentleman, dissatisfied with the commonly received notion concerning this word TASCIA, has proposed an opinion of his own, which I shall here report (and the rather, as it seems not to be generally known) with a short confutation. He inclines to look out for the name of some

(1) Wise, p. 225.
(2) Idem, p. 226. bis.
(3) Camden, col. CXIII.
(4) Plott, Nat. Hist. Oxfordsh. p. 312, seq. Univ. Hist. XIX. p. 129. and in Not.
(5) Tacitus, Vit. Agric. c. 13.

people

COINS OF CUNOBELIN. 33

people or state in that term; and in Pliny III. c. 4. he finds Tascodunitari, Cononienses, a people of Gallia Narbonensis, which father Harduin from the MSS. reads Tascoduni Tarueonienses, and therefore he conjectures CVNOBELIN TASCIO may perhaps mean Cunobelin Tascodunorum (1). But this does not appear to me to be what they call a happy conjecture; for tho' 'tis more than probable the Gauls had a species of money not greatly unlike our British pieces (2), and Peireskius informed Mr. Camden they had such (3); yet this does not affect either our British coins in general, or those with TASCIO in particular, because, in some of these coins, as in classes third and fourth, the name of CVNOBELIN is actually joined with TASCIO, or some of its abbreviations; and yet this King had nothing to do with any state or people of Gallia Narbonensis. And we know of no place of the like found in that part of this island where he is supposed to have reigned.

But have you, methinks I hear your Lordship say, any thing more plausible to offer than the notions you have been exploding? That, my Lord, is as it may prove; for here, and in this respect, I find myself exactly in the same circumstances with these learned men. The subject is very remote in time, is dark and difficult in itself, and has been rendered more so by the preceding conjectures. Conjecture, to say truth, reasonable and well founded, is all that can be tendered in the case, and consequently is the most that can be expected from me; and as I have a con-

(1) Wise. p. 227.
(2) Montfaucon III. p. 56.
(3) Camd. col. CIX.

F ception,

ception, which appears to me to be of this sort. I shall produce it to your Lordship, though with all becoming diffidence, submitting it, as I freely do, to your Lordship's candour and decision.

To begin then; it appears from the irrefragable testimony of Julius Cæsar, when rightly understood (for the passage has been strangely perverted and mistaken by many) that before his arrival in Britain, the inhabitants of the island had no coined money amongst them. For the account he gives of this matter, even after his second expedition, is this: " Utuntur aut ære, aut taleis ferreis " ad certum pondus examinatis, pro nummo (1)." This Bishop Gibson in Camden renders, " The money used by " the Britains is brass, or iron rings, at a certain weight, " instead of it (2)." Professor Duncan thus: " They " use brass money, and iron rings of a certain weight (3)." and Mr. Borlase to the same effect: " The Britons use " either brass money, or iron tallies instead of money (4)." These gentlemen appear to me to follow an old discarded reading, *autem nummo æreo*. The case is plain in respect to Mr. Borlase, tho' not of Mr. Duncan, who therefore is the more to be blamed; however, they all restrain the word *examinatis* to the *annuli*, or *taleæ*, or *laminæ*, the things last mentioned, by which means they give us

---

(1) Cæsar de B. G. v. c. 12. This is a much controverted passage in respect of the reading; but the three best editions of Dr. Davies, Dr. Clarke, and Professor Oudendorp, all agree in reading *aut ære*, or *autem ære*, which is the only part of the sentence I am concerned with here.

(2) Camden col. XLI.

(3) Duncan's translation of Cæsar's Commentaries, Lond. 1755. 2 vol. 8vo.

(4) Borlase, Antiq. of Cornwall, p. 249. See him again, p. 253, 254.

COINS OF CUNOBELIN. 35

to underſtand, that the Britons at this time, according to Cæſar, were really poſſeſſed of braſs money (1). But with all due ſubmiſſion to theſe great men, this paſſage of Cæſar ought to be tranſlated thus: " For money, they " uſed either pieces of braſs, or iron tallies, adjuſted to a " certain weight," meaning, that the pieces of braſs were unſtamped, as well as the iron tallies, and only reduced to ſome certain ſtandard in reſpect of weight; for the word *examinatis* refers both to the pieces of braſs and the iron tallies. The former were conſequently blank; and indeed, had the Britons known how to have given them an impreſſion, no valid reaſon can be aſſigned, why they did not ſtamp their iron alſo (2). Beſides, it is well known, that the firſt money was in this rude condition in other countries as well as Britain, and was eſtimated by weight (3).

Caſſivellaunus was the Prince whom Cæſar had chiefly to deal with, and therefore whoever maturely conſiders the teſtimony here adduced, and the ſenſe I have given it, will have abundant reaſon to ſuſpect that our antiquaries, Speed (4), Plott (5), Walker (6), Lhuyd (7), and Borlaſe (8), muſt be miſtaken in appropriating coins to him,

---

(1) And yet Mr. Camden himſelf is of a different opinion. See him, col. CCCLII.
(2) For that they could do this, ſeems plain from that iron piece in Mr. Thoreſby's Muſeum, p. 337.
(3) Wiſe, p. 217. Borlaſe, p. 257. Thoreſby, p. 279. Walker in Camd. col. CXIV. &c. &c. &c.
(4) Speed, Hiſt. p. 48. See alſo Camden, col. CXV.
(5) Dr. Plott's Oxfordſh. p. 312, 313.
(6) Ob. Walker in Camd. col. CXVI.
(7) Præf. to his Archæologia, in Lewis's Hiſt. of Britain, p. 62.
(8) Borlaſe, p. 251, 260.

the Britons in his days having no coined money; not of gold, certainly, as the pieces in question are. Mr. Wife, I observe, and Bishop Nicholson (1), and Mr. Morton (2), all agree with me in this; and the first notes, in respect of CAS (the letters that appear upon one of these coins) "ad "Castellanos, vel Cascantes Hispaniæ, Cassios Britanniæ, "vel ad Cassinomagum Galliæ, æquo jure pertinent." But as there is a figure on horseback upon these coins, I rather think it to be a regal one; not Cassivellaun's, but Cunobelin's; the coin being mis-read, as will be noted hereafter. At present I only remark, that these conjectures of Mr. Wife only account for the inscription on one of the coins; to wit, CAS, and not for CASCO the legend on the other, which does not so well consist with Castellani, Cascantes, &c. But to proceed with the antiquaries, Speed, Plott, &c.: It must be remembered that these coins are gold, which was not discovered in this island in Cæsar's time, as is evident from his silence in the Commentaries, and the express testimony of Cicero in his Epistles (3), though it was found soon after (4). I mention this particular in respect of the gold coins of Cunobelin, as likewise of Mr. Wife; who observes, concerning the coins of this Prince, that they are gold and silver, and yet Cæsar testifies the British money was brass; but certainly, tho' before Cæsar, and in Cassivellaun's time, the

(1) Nicholson, Hist. Lib.
(2) Morton, N. H. of Northamptonsh. cited by Borlase, p. 250.
(3) Cicero, Epist. ad Fam. VII. 7. ad Attic. IV. 15.
(4) Strabo IV. p. 199. Tacit. Vit. Agric. c. 12. See Dr. Plott, Oxfordsh. p. 164. and Mr. Borlase, p. 253.
(5) Wife, p. 226.

British

COINS OF CUNOBELIN. 37

British specie, such as it was, might be only brass or iron tallies adjusted to weight, there might be both gold and silver money in Cunobelin's reign. But now, that I may observe this by the way, the invention or appearance of gold here, so immediately after, seems to exclude the notion of those who think the gold specie found here, might be brought from Spain, or Africa, countries abounding with this metal (1). But what is more decisive, the legend of the coin, class. V. no. II. is TASCO (2), and not CAS, and the first letter in Speed's original type is a T; so that the truth of the inscription is TASCO, that is, TASCIO. And whereas the coin produced by Mr. Walker in Camden, class. V. no. 3. has CAS only, 'tis clear to me, that this piece, which was Mr. William Charleton's (3), is the very same with the former, the legend being imperfectly given, and the reverse the same as in Speed, whereas in Camden it is inverted or turned upside down. There is room apparently for the rest of the letters on the obverse, which possibly were either obliterated in Mr. Charleton's coin, or were overlooked by the antiquary, Walker, or his engraver, or both. As to the first letter, which in this coin is so plainly c, there is some confusion in this part of the piece, as will appear by comparing the type of this coin with that of the other. However, as in Charleton's piece it is c, this convinces me of the existence of the cross stroke of the T; and indeed it is plain to be seen in Speed's original type, tho' it be omitted in the copy of it in Camden. Speed's coin was

(1) Wise, p. 227.
(2) Mr. Morton's scov, reported by Borlase, p. 251, is most ridiculous.
(3) Camden, col. CXCIX.

certainly

certainly more perfect than Charleton's; and what the horseman has in his hand is evidently there a whip. If these things are so, this gold coin (for the two coins are now reduced to one) is in all probability a piece of Cunobelin's, his mark TASCIO appearing upon it; and I have accordingly registered it as such in the 5th class.

Mr. Speed has a notion that Comius, mentioned in Cæsar, and his associate in the invasion of our island, was King of the Attrebates in Britain (1); and he is followed in this by Mr. Borlase (2). These authors consequently, ascribing to him the gold coin in Camden 1, 10, must be of opinion, the Britons were in possession of the art of coining before Cæsar's time, or at least in his days. Now, that the coin belongs to this person, and that there were a people in Britain of this name, will be readily granted; but that Comius was King of them may be justly doubted, since he rather appears to have been King of the Attrebates on the continent of Gaul. This Comius, as it appears from Cæsar, was with him in Gaul before his first expedition, and was even constituted by him King of the Attrebates (3), who, as Cæsar had not as yet set his foot in Britain, must in all reason be the Attrebates of Gaul; they certainly could be no other, since he says, *they were already conquered* (4). Cæsar again tells us, how greatly he was at a loss to get the proper informations concerning the extent of the island of Britain, what nations inhabited it, what experience they

(1) Speed, Hist. p. 29. seq.
(2) Borlase, p. 250, 256.
(3) Cæs. de B. G. IV. c. 21.
(4) And see him, Lib. II.

had

COINS OF CUNOBELIN. 39

had in war, by what laws they were governed, and what kind of havens they had, " quæ omnia, says he, fere " Gallis erant incognita:" In short, he was forced to dispatch C. Volusenus to reconnoitre, and procure him the best intelligence he could as to these matters; but certainly he could not have been so much distressed on these points, nor have been obliged to convene the Gaulish merchants for the obtaining of their assistance therein, if Comius had been King of the British Attrebates, who were seated far in the island; in Berkshire according to Camden, and in Oxfordshire if we follow Mr. Baxter. But the coin itself being gold, methinks, puts this matter out of all doubt, for from thence we may assuredly infer, that, if Cæsar is to be believed, it cannot be a British piece, and consequently must be a Gallic coin.

But perhaps it may be alledged, that the Britons had some trade, which cannot well be conducted without money. This is in a good measure the notion of Mr. Wise, in respect of our Britons, " Ante Romanorum in " Britanniam adventum, says he, quali moneta usi sunt " incolæ, haud facile dictu est, et gentem cum exteris mer- " caturam exercentem monetæ usus nullo modo effugere " posset (1)." However, he appears afterwards to be of the same opinion with us, that the Aborigines of Britain had no coined money of their own; for he says, " Nullus " credo Britannos, vel ante, vel post subactam insulam, " monetam propriam signatam habuisse (2)," implying, they might make use of a specie, tho' not of their own fabrication; but even this is more than necessary in the

(1) Wise, p. 225.
(2) Idem, p. 226.

case,

case, since traffic and commerce can be in some imperfect degree carried on without money, as it is at this day in many parts of the world (1). The Phœnicians, 'tis thought, had no coined money till the time of Alexander the Great (2); the case was much the same with the Hebrews (3); that the Britons should therefore be without money, is not so strange as Walker represents it (4). Toland says, speaking of the Hebrides or Hebudes in his time, "The use of money is still in some of those islands "unknown, and till a few ages past in all of them (5)." I add, that the Britons in the Eastern and South-Eastern parts of the island, where Cassivellaun and Cunobelin resided, had in appearance no other trade at this time, but some inconsiderable dealings with the Gauls (6). The case might be very different in the West.

Ed. Lhuyd thought the Britons had gold coins before the coming of the Romans, "because there have been "found thick pieces of that metal, hollowed on one side, "with variety of unintelligible marks and characters upon "them. And the reason why he thought they were "coined before the Romans came, is this: If the Britons "had learned the art from them, they would (tho' never "so inartificially) have endeavoured to imitate their man-"ner of coins; and, in all likelihood, have added letters, "and the head of their Kings (7)." It may be replied,

(1) Borlase, Antiq. p. 250, 256.
(2) Wise, p. 217.
(3) Conringius de Numm. Hebræor. Paradoxa, p. 163.
(4) Walker in Camd. col. CXIV.
(5) Toland, Misc. Works, p. 176.
(6) Cæf. B. G. IV. 20. Strabo, Lib. IV.
(7) Lhuyd in Nicholson, p. 30. and in Camd. col. 774

1st. That the Britons had then no gold amongst them. 2dly. In Bishop Nicholson's words, " 'tis against the ex-"press testimony of Julius Cæsar, who could hardly be "imposed on in this part of the account he gives of our "isle." 3dly. We think they sufficiently resemble the Roman coins, both in their manner, the letters, and the heads, a point which will at large be made good below.

Montfaucon thinks the Gauls had money before Cæsar's time (1); and many authors, I find, imagine the Britons had (2), as has been in part remarked above; but I shall rest this matter on what has been said.

My next position is, that if afterwards, and before the reign of Cunobelin, the Britons paid any *vectigal* to the Romans, which perhaps may be doubted (3), such *vectigal* was not discharged in coin, but in commodities of various kinds. This, it is allowed, is not of equal certainty with the former assertion, but will be thought exceeding probable on the footing of what has been alledged above (4).

I observe thirdly, what I think can hardly be controverted, that the coins of Cunobelin are all of them the workmanship, either of a Roman master, or of some artist of the province of Gaul, sufficiently expert in the business of coining, and well versed in the Roman customs, their theology and mythology in particular. This, I think, appears evidently from the following particulars.

(1) Montf. III. p. 57.
(2) Borlase, p. 249, 257.
(3) I say this, because the Britons were no more always punctual to their engagements, than the Gauls.
(4) Page 28.

First,

First, The deities that appear on these coins are altogether Roman; Janus (1), for example, was no British deity, but a Roman one. Mr. Sammes, indeed, esteems him a God of the Britons from this coin (2); but it cannot be inferred solely from the type of this piece, that Janus was a British deity, since, if the artist was a Roman, or a provincial, the bust may exhibit the Janus of the Latins, represented here, because he was the first that coined brass money (3), of which metal this piece consists. If this was some of the first money that was struck in the island, as I imagine it might, nothing could be more natural, nor at the same time more ingenious, than to place the head of this Roman deity upon it. This, I think, accounts better for the appearance of the *Bifrons* on this coin, than Mr. Camden's and Alford's notion does, who were of opinion this head was impressed, because Britain began, at that time, to be a little refined from its barbarity; for Janus is said to have first changed barbarity into humanity, and for that reason to be painted with two faces (4). I prefer it also to the suggestion of Mr. Walker, that it may allude to the shutting of Janus's temple by Augustus. Alford produces a third reason for the head of Janus appearing on this British coin:
" Romulus et Tatius, inito fœdere, Jano templum po-
" nentes, duas illi facies effinxere, quo duorum regum &
" populorum coitionem, & unitatem corporis innuerent.
" Cunobelinus itaque eo argumento voluit ostendere

(1) Camd. I. 1. and Lord Pemb. Plate II. Tab. 94. and 95.
(2) Sammes, p. 139.
(3) Montf. I. p. 16.
(4) Camd. ad hunc Nummum. Alford, p. 5.

" Britanniam

" Britanniam Romæ conjunctam, et illius imperii provin-
" vinciam esse (1)." But there is no occasion for this far-
fetched surmise; however, it should be noted, that Mr.
Walker doubts whether the bicipital figure be a Janus,
the heads of this deity being diverse, one old, the other
young, whereas " this seems, he says, made for two young
" women's faces; whether Cunobelin's wives, or sisters,
" or children, I know not (2)." This, it must be allowed, is well observed; for the heads of Janus are, in a
general way, either both of them bearded, or one bearded
and the other smooth: But yet there is no great weight
in the remark, because, as appears from Montfaucon (3),
and Lord Pembroke, Part II. pl. 84. the heads of Janus
are sometimes represented without a beard (4). But what
inclines me to think the head of Janus has a relation to
the coinage, is, that in the very next coin in Camden, a
brass coin of Cunobelin's likewise, you have the mint-
master at work; a circumstance which makes it more
than probable, that the head of Janus on the piece in
question, has some allusion to the art of coining.

The next deity I mention is Apollo, who is here represented playing on his harp (5); an attitude and attribute which plainly determines him to be the Roman
Apollo. Belus, or Belinus, the Apollo of the Britons
and Gauls, had no connexion with music, that we know
of; his presidency in this art being the imagination of the

(1) Alford, p. 5.
(2) It may be observed here, that the Muse Thalia, who doubtless had
no beard, is represented with two faces. Montf. L p. 70.
(3) L p. 18.
(4) See also Lord Pembr. Part II. pl. 95. no. 5.
(5) Class IV. no. 1. and 3.

Greeks and Romans (1). Cunobelin is supposed to take his name from this deity (2), Cuno signifying, as the etymologists will tell you, the same as King or Prince (3): Apollo was therefore, probably, a favourite idol with him. If Apollo was any thing more than the sun, he was the deity that cured diseases (4).

To Apollo I may subjoin the goddess of Victory, who is commonly delineated cloathed, in full length, and with wings, upon the Roman coins, as here (5). The Britons indeed had a deity called Andraste, or Andate (6), of much the same character as the Roman Victoria (7); but her figure was probably frightful and truculent, and very unlike this. Mr. Baxter, after giving a most shocking etym. of her name, says, " Andrastæ autem isti Britanni " veteres humanas hostias immaniter immolabant, ritu ve- " tusto, quam et ante commissum cum Romanis prælium " Amazonis nostra Vondica precibus invocabat horrendis, " uti memoriæ prodidit Dion (8)." There is a bust of Victory on two of these old British coins (9), and Mr. Camden says he had seen the same figure of her on the Ro-

(1) I differ from Hearne here, who, in Lel. Itin. VIII. p.20. thinks it was out of devotion to Apollo, that the antient Britons delighted so much in the harp.

(2) Camden, col. CX. Alford, p. 4. And Mr. Baxter, Gl. p. 94. deviates not far, " Cunobelinus, hoc est, *Cond velin, Capite flavo*, sive 'Hʌũŋʜ : " nam de *Bél* sive *Belin*, *Sole*, flavus color et *melin* et *velin* dicitur."

(3) Camden, col. CXI. Baxter, in Gl. p. 94. bis, esteems it the Brit. *Cond*, Caput. See also Hearne in Alford, p. 5. Pettingal, p. 4.

(4) Cæsf. VI. c. 17.
(5) Class II. no. 3.
(6) A corruption, according to Baxter, of the other.
(7) Camd. col. CXI. and XLIII.
(8) Baxt. Gl. p. 16. seq.
(9) Camd. l. no. 12. class III. no. 7.

man

man coins; but for my part, I do not remember any such. The first of these is no coin of Cunobelin's, but the second is, and in my opinion may serve to convince us, that the British Andate corresponded but in part with the Roman Victory. The Grecian Hercules, with his club, succeeds Victory, class I. no. 2. for what he carries on his shoulder is a club, as is evident from the type of the similar coin in Lord Pembroke's collection, where it is plainly knotted. But what best establishes this, my Lord, is class IV. no. 5. where Hercules stands at full length, as here, with his club and the lion's skin. I call this the Grecian, or, if your Lordship pleases, the Roman Hercules, on account of the club and the lion's skin; for tho', according to Lucian, Hercules Ogmius, a deity of the Gauls, had his club, and the spoils of the lion (1), yet that was probably a later portrait of him, after the Gauls became acquainted with the Greek and Roman mythology; but be that as it will, the Britons of the age cannot be thought to have any knowledge of the Grecian Hercules, and his exploits: for tho' Richard of Cirencester, p. 9. mentions Hercules amongst the British deities, it was because of his introduction in after times. Lucian, methinks, plainly intimates that these attributes belong to the Grecian Hercules; for he thought, he says, the Gauls might represent him in the manner they did, to ridicule the gods of the Greeks; and in Montf. II. p. 271. the Gallic Hercules is naked. And I am of opinion, that the Gallic (2) and Belgic (3) representation of Her-

(1) Lucian II. p. 365. Ed. Amst. 1687.
(2) Montf. II. p. 272.
(3) Montf. II. p. 283.

cules,

cules, with the club, and the spoils of the lion, are both of them owing to their acquaintance with the Roman mythology, the letters and formulæ of the latter appearing on one of those monuments; we therefore cannot esteem them pure Gallic remains.

In class III. no. 2. and in one of Lord Pembroke's, class II. no. 6. we have actually the Pegasus, a creature of meer Greek and Roman imagination, connected with Parnassus and the Muses, of whom these distant and unpolished islanders could have no knowledge of themselves. Mr. Camden mistakes the Pegasus on this coin for a simple horse; however, he makes us amends, by mentioning another coin he had seen with a Pegasus.

But what is yet more extraordinary, we have in class III. no. 3. and 7. a Theban Sphinx, with wings, another phantastical being, unknown, for any thing that appears, to the antient Britons, but assumed, as is most probable, by Cunobelin and his artist, out of compliment to Augustus Cæsar; who, as Suetonius tells us, used the Sphinx on a seal (1). This creature of the brain is seen also on a coin in Montfaucon's second class of the Gallic coins, and was probably adopted on the same respectful account. The Sphinx also belongs to Mars (2), and therefore is very properly joined with Victory in our third class, no. 7. And as Camulus, towards whom Cunobelin seems to have borne uncommon respect, by naming his royal seat Camulodunum from him, is but another name for Mars, there may have been a double reason for his taking the Sphinx for one of his devices.

(1) Sueton. Aug. c. 50. Pliny, N. H. XXXVII. 1.
(2) Gent. Magazine, 1752, p. 406, 407.

COINS OF CUNOBELIN. 47

The 4th of the IVth clafs prefents us, laftly, with a very perfect and fine Centaur winding his horn, another Grecian conceit, brought hither from Rome. In regard to thefe Roman deities in general, the cafe of the Britons was much the fame with that of the Gauls; for thefe laft, as appears from Montfaucon (1), borrowed the Roman deities, and their attributes, as foon as they became acquainted with that people. Matters went the fame way at Carthage (2).

What I would notice next is the manner, the tafte, and the execution of thefe coins of Cunobelin, all which are entirely Roman (3). This is acknowledged by the authors of the Univerfal Hiftory, vol. XIX. p. 130. as likewife by Mr. Baxter (4); though Mr. Lhuyd above feems to difpute it: In fhort, thefe coins are very terfe and elegant; and if your Lordfhip will pleafe to compare them with thofe in Camden's fecond table, with fome in the firft, and with the Gallic coins in Montfaucon, you will inftantly be fenfible they are the productions of fome fkilful artift, inftead of a clumfy barbarian. The Britons certainly knew nothing of crowns and laurels, whence therefore could the laureate head come, in clafs V. no. 1. and clafs III. no. ult. and the laureate crown, in clafs III. no. 2. but either immediately or mediately from Rome? Mr. Camden is of opinion, and with great appearance of probability, that the coin in clafs V. no. 1. reprefents the head of Auguftus; and who will not from

(1) Tom. II. Book V.
(2) ———— p. 282.
(3) See clafs II. no. 1. III. no. 1. I. no. 1. IV. no. 1, &c. &c. &c.
(4) Baxter, Gloff. voce TASCIA, cited above.

thence

thence conclude, in conjunction with the goodnefs of the work on both fides, that it muft be the atchievement of a Roman, or at leaft a Romaniz'd hand? In clafs VI. no. 2. and clafs V. no. 2. which are both gold coins, you have very elegant horfes mounted with riders, and fcarce are there any better on the Roman denarii of the times.

It may be of weight in the argument to obferve, that the deities of the antient Britons, who were grofly and foully immerfed in idolatry (1), were monfters of uglinefs and deformity, as we are exprefly informed by Gildas, whofe words fhall be adduced below. But now, if thefe coins had been the work of the natives, and not of a foreign mafter, your Lordfhip may depend upon it we fhould fee the reprefentation of fome of their mif-fhapen idols upon them; which is fo far from being the cafe, that, on the contrary, every thing here is proportionable and agreeable to the eye, and not one of thofe hideous and portentous figures appears: the fubjects are really Roman, and the tafte and manner of the figures and reprefentations the fame.

I add, in the laft place, the form of the letters, which are clearly and inconteftably no other than Roman. It has been queftioned by fome, whether the Britons had any letters before Julius Cæfar came amongft them, notwithstanding what the Oxford antiquaries pretend (2); but if they had, there is no reafon to think they were of the Roman caft (3); they would probably have more re-

(1) Ufher, Brit. Ecclef. Antiq. p. 1.
(2) Wood, Hift. Antiq. L. c. 1, 2, 3. Lel. Itin. IV. p. 156, 168.
(3) Wife, p. 276.

fembled

COINS OF CUNOBELIN. 49

sembled the Greek (1), or the oriental, according to Mr. Sammes (2), or the old British (3), commonly called the Saxon. But now, instead of this, you have almost a complete Roman alphabet on the British coins.

A B C D E G H I L M N O P R S T V X.

This is certainly very remarkable, and may convince any unprejudiced person, that the coins of Cunobelin, on which most of these letters, 13 out of 18, appear (letters of this form, and no other) especially if you consider them as a first essay (which is the light in which I view them) must almost necessarily be the work of a provincial, or other Roman master. Here I may likewise mention the word æ as part of REX, in class III. no. 5. as also the latinized form of the King's name, CVNOBELINVS, on that coin. But to return to the letters; this matter has long been thought an affair of difficulty amongst our antiquaries (4), and can be solv'd upon no other supposition so reasonably, as that a Roman artist was employed in striking the coins at first.

The several particulars here mentioned, my Lord, amount in the whole to this; that a Roman hand of some sort was employed in the first British mints. But you will ask, how could this happen, since, after the recess of Julius Cæsar, the Romans never approached Britain, till A. Plautius came hither with the Legions, in the reign of the Emperor Claudius? I answer, tho' no military force

(1) Cæf. de B. G. VI. c. 14. and Oudendorp ad loc.
(2) See his Brit. Antiq. Illustr. passim.
(3) Ed. Lhuyd's Preface in Lewis's Hist. of Britain, p. 60. seq.
(4) Ibid.

H   entered

entered the island in that interval, it does not follow but many individuals might; wherefore, could it be shewn, that a continual intercourse and friendship between the two people, the Britons and Romans, were cultivated in the intermediate space, it will appear probable, that in fact many Romans did arrive.

This, my Lord, would be made out in very few words, if Cunobelin, as it is delivered by Jeffrey of Monmouth (1), and Guido de Columna, who have been followed by other authors (2), was educated at Rome; or if, as Walker and Alford tell us (3), he was the son or nephew of Mandubratius, the friend of Julius Cæsar, who restored him to the government of the Trinobantes, and even carried him with him to Rome (4). But I doubt these facts are infinitely too precarious to be relied on; since the antients, Suetonius, Tacitus, and Dio, take no notice of them. We must therefore look out for something more substantial. Now Strabo says, he had seen some British youths at Rome, that were half a foot higher than the tallest men (5). Julius Cæsar carried with him some British captives (6), but these could not be the young men intended by Strabo; for in his time they must have been

(1) Galfr. Monum. IV. c. xi.
(2) Fabian, fol. XVIII. b. Speed, p. 31. Alford I. p. 4. Walker in Camd. col. CIX, CXV, CXXV. In col. CXVI. he says, " He, meaning Cunobelin, " lived in Rome, in favour with Augustus and the Senate, who declared " him *a friend of the Romans*, as is plainly intimated in that speech of the " generous Caractacus." But I find nothing in Caractacus's speech that implies this.
(3) Walker, in Camd. col. CXVI. Alford, p. 2.
(4) Cæf. de B. G. V. c. 20, 22.
(5) Strabo, Lib. IV. p. 200.
(6) Cæf. de B. G. V. c. 23.

COINS OF CUNOBELIN.   51

too old to be called ἀντίπαιδες. The same author tells us again, that in his time, certain of the *Reguli* of Britain obtained, by embassies and acts of civility, the friendship of Augustus Cæsar, dedicated their presents in the Capitol, and brought almost the whole island into a state of familiarity with the Romans (1). Cunobelin, one has reason to think, was principal amongst these petty Kings; and the British Envoys, no doubt, were wrapt in admiration, on beholding the grandeur and magnificence of the city of Rome; were transported with pleasure, on seeing their manners and customs so totally different from theirs, and at the same time so polite and genteel. They probably would not be least taken with the beauty and excellency of the Roman money, gold, silver, and brass, impressed with such a variety of instructing devices, so masterly performed. These things they would naturally speak of on their return home, and with exaggeration, as usually happens in these cases, rather than diminution. The author says further, that in this reign, the Romans had not imposed upon the Britons any tribute, or other heavy customs; and the imposts laid upon their exports and imports, were easily paid by the Britons, being but trifling payments, and for a species of merchandise of no great value. Matters between the two people were not always, 'tis true, upon the same amicable footing, for Augustus entertained a design, more than once, of invading them (2): and when on a time he had advanced as far as Gaul, the Britons sent Ambassadors to him to sue for peace, which was granted them, " upon their

(1) Strabo, l. c.
(2) Hor. Od. I. 35. III. 5. IV. 14.

" promising,

"promising, say the authors of the Univerſal Hiſtory, to
"ſtand to their agreement with his predeceſſor Julius."
Mr. Carte thinks this expedition of Auguſtus was for the
purpoſe of regulating the payment (1). The political
ſentiments of Auguſtus Cæſar were afterwards not to en-
large the empire, but to let the ocean be the bounds of
it, as nature ſeemed to direct; at preſent, 'tis plain, he
had different notions; quære, therefore, whether his de-
ſign now was not to penetrate further into the iſland, and
to conciliate and gain to his intereſt the more diſtant
clans.

Let this matter be as it will, the Britons behaved in a
complying and moſt engaging manner under Tiberius, the
next Emperor, when Cunobelin was ſtill living; for their
Reguli, or petty Princes, were then ſo well affected to the
Romans, as to ſend back ſome of Germanicus's ſoldiers
that had been ſhipwrecked on their coaſts (2). This
ſhipwreck probably happened on the coaſt of Norfolk
or Suffolk, amongſt the *Iceni*, ſubject to Cunobelin, as
will be ſeen hereafter; and thoſe ſubaltern Princes were
conſequently the dependents of Cunobelin, and acted in
this matter by his direction. Mr. Carte further ſays,
" The principal of the Britiſh nobility reſorted frequently
" to Rome itſelf, and ſome of them were there edu-
" cated (3)." So ſay alſo Matth. of Weſtm. (4), and
Alford (5); but I doubt they have no good authority for
this.

(1) Carte, I. p. 97.
(2) Tacitus, Annal. II. c. 24.
(3) Carte, I. p. 97.
(4) M. Weſtm. p. 51.
(5) Alford, p. 15.

COINS OF CUNOBELIN.

In Caligula's time, Cunobelin being yet on the throne, the friendship and familiarity between the Britons and Romans still subsisted; for Adminius, the son of Cunobelin, being driven from home by his father, fled to Caligula with a few partizans, as to a friend (1), just as Bericus and others afterwards reforted to Rome to the Emperor Claudius (2); and Suetonius, signifying the cause of this Emperor's attempt upon Britain, says, the island was at this time very seditious, *ob non redditos transfugas* (3); which implies, not only that Adminius and Bericus, but many others, had of late time taken refuge at Rome (4). It appears from Tacitus, that Venusius, *e Jugantum civitate*, or *Brigantum*, as some emend it (5), was very friendly disposed towards the Roman interest, when they afterwards invaded the island under Claudius (6): and Mr. Horseley thinks the *Iceni* had entered into amity with the Romans, even from the time of Julius Cæsar (7); and this is the opinion also of Mr. Baxter, " Credibile est " Icenos veteris Britanniæ populos, amicitia usos Roma-" norum frænandis Belgis *Primæ Britanniæ* populis, qui-" buscum solis Cæsar bellum gesserat. Belgo-Brigantes " isti, ut verisimile videtur, dudum Belgarum jugum ex-" cusserant, creato sibi Silure Pendragone (8)." But

---

(1) Suetonius in Caio, c. 44.
(2) Dio, Lib. LX. Horseley thinks he may be the same with Adminius, or one of his companions.
(3) M. Westm. insinuates, that Claudius's invasion was owing to Guiderius, or Togodumnus, refusing to pay the usual tribute, p. 45, 46.
(4) Suet. in Claud. c. 17.
(5) Horseley, p. 26. Pettingal, p. 5.
(6) Annal. XII. c. 40.
(7) Horseley, p. 36.
(8) Baxter, Gloss. voc. CUNOBELINUS. CARTISMANDUA. ICENI.

without

without running this detail into any greater length, the appearance of Auguftus's head on one of thefe coins, and the Sphinx upon others, are a clear and convincing evidence of the regard and veneration in which Cunobelin held that Emperor; wherefore it may reafonably be affumed, that there is no abfurdity, no impropriety, no improbability, in fuppofing him to procure and employ a Roman mafter in the bufinefs of his mints. It was very natural for him to think of ftamping money, as he had heard, and no doubt faw, the Romans did (for I muft think the Ambaffadors above fpoken of, would unqueftionably bring fome of the Roman fpecie with them into Britain); and for that purpofe would probably get the affiftance of one of their artifts, by inviting him into Britain. From hence, I am perfuaded, proceeded the compliments made to Auguftus upon Cunobelin's coins, together with that variety of other matter, favouring of the Roman religion, their manner and tafte, fo confpicuous on the Britifh coins, and in particular, their alphabet. Thefe things feem not to be eafily accounted for, on any other fuppofition: for my part, if TASCIO, or TASCIA, could pafs for a Roman name, which I much queftion, both on account of itfelf, as likewife becaufe a Prænomen, or an Agnomen, has never once been feen with it on thefe coins, I fhould think he was really an Italian, or a gremial of Rome; as it is, I take him to have been a provincial of the Roman province in Gaul, educated and inftructed, as well in the art of coining, as in the other Roman arts, and more efpecially in all matters relative to their mythology. The mint-mafters of thefe times were people of confequence; fuch were the IIIViri and the IIIIViri Monetales at Rome,

Rome, whose names we see so frequently on the Consular coins. And I need only remit your Lordship to Stosch (1), for a proof of the great artists of Greece putting their names on the gems. As for the coins, we see the masters soon after placing their names very generally upon those of the West; I speak not of the Roman specie, but the Saxon and Francic; a custom which perhaps might be borrowed from the practice and example of TASCIO, on this British money, the Gauls on the continent fetching much more important matters and customs from our island. In short, the British mints, of which I suppose there might be several, were all, as I apprehend, under the care and inspection of TASCIO, the mint-master of Cunobelin; and this will account for his name appearing upon pieces coined at different places; as at Verulam, Camulodunum, &c. as also for pieces of this King struck at other places, and of equal goodness in the work, tho' the name of TASCIO does not occur upon them. Mr. Wise has been pleased to mention the Tascodumni, as a people of Gallia Narbonensis; and if he, or any other person, should incline to think TASCIO might be of that nation, and the name at length might be written Tascodumnus, I have no objection.

This, my Lord, is my opinion concerning the word TASCIO on these coins; and the sense I have here affixed to it, and the other notions and particulars I have advanced above, lead me naturally into a persuasion, that the coins of all the six classes are the productions of Tascio, a provincial artist, entertained in the service of the British Prince Cunobelin; and moreover, that they are

(1) Amstel. 1724, fol.

the

the first fruits, and perhaps the last, of the British mints, meaning those that were wrought and employed before the reign of the Emperor Claudius, and his conquests; and lastly, that this money was not by any means made for the purpose of paying tribute, but to be the general and current specie of the subjects of Cunobelin. This hypothesis, for I dare not call it by any higher name, sufficiently solves all the appearances on the coins themselves, and is withal consistent with the several notices which the antients have left us, concerning the pecuniary matters of this island in those remote times. It comports also with that circumstance, thought so extraordinary, of our finding no coins of Adminius, Caractacus, Togodumnus, &c. since, these being contemporaries with Claudius (the two latter at least) it seems never to have been in their power to strike any money.

Mr. Camden has given us a coin with a Greek inscription, ΒΡΕΤΑΝΝΙΚΟΣ. on obv. ΜΗΤΡΟΠΟΛΙΣ ΕΤΙΜΙΝΑΙΟΥ on the reverse (1). The piece is well known, and needs no further description: By Britannicus, he understands the son of Claudius Cæsar, honoured by a decree of the Senate, with the surname Britannicus, and then writes, " Who this Etiminius should be, does not ap-
" pear to me, unless we imagine him to be that Admi-
" nius, Cunobelin's son, who, as Suetonius says, took
" protection under C. Caligula (2)." But we are by no means sure that Adminius was living, when the Emperor Claudius, on his return to Rome, from his British expedition, was honoured with a triumph; and both he

(1) Camd. Num. Rom. Tab. I. no. 3. Speed, p. 55.
(2) And so Speed, p. 55.

and

COINS OF CUNOBELIN.

and his son were invested with the title of Britannicus (1). However, the illustrious Spanheim has shewn, that this Greek coin belongs to a very different country; but the whole of this affair has been so fully stated by Mr. Carte (2), that I need not any longer to detain your Lordship with it.

As to Caratacus; the coin with CEARATIC, conjectured to belong to him, and engraved here as one of Cunobelin's (3), will be mentioned below more than once. All therefore I shall need to note further, will be in relation to two pieces supposed to belong to Arviragus, and another which has been thought the property of Bericus. The Poet Juvenal has these words,

> Regem aliquem capies, vel de temone Britanno
> Excidet Arviragus.
>
> Sat. IV. 126.

Whence the Monkish authors have got the name of Arviragus, a British Prince (4), and have related great matters concerning him, notwithstanding the silence of Tacitus, Dio, &c. And Alford, the Popish annalist, to salve the credit of his friends the Monks, pretends, that Caratacus and Arviragus were one and the same person (5). But the best judges, my Lord, are of opinion, that Arviragus, in that passage of Juvenal, is not a proper name,

(1) Dio, Lib. LX. p. 781.
(2) Carte, p. 98. in Not.
(3) Class VI. no. 2.
(4) Galfr. Monum. IV. c. 16. Matth. West. p. 51. alii. Abp. Usher also, p. 12. and 288. esteems him a real person, and Camden col. XXXVII.
(5) Alford, p. 6, 22, 23.

I but

but an appellative. Thus Mr. Baxter, "ARVIRAGUS, apud
" fatyricum Juvenalem viri nomen non eft, quod vel ip-
" fius poetæ verfus fubindicat:——

"Regem aliquem, &c.

" Diverfum quid igitur *Arviragus* a Rege. Certè *Ardh*
" *rig*, vel altera etiam dialecto *Ardh rag*, ut et *Kend rig*
" (vitiofe Romanorum ore *Arviragus* et *Cingetorix)*
" Dictator erat a communi Gallorum Britannorumque,
" Concilio bellorum temporibus fummæ rerum præ-
" fectus, &c. (1)." This notion of Mr. Baxter's, I find,
is approved both by Mr. Wife (2), and others (3); and
Mr. Carte concurs with them, tho' he varies fomething as
to the etymon, " *Arviragus*, a latinized word for *Ard-*
" *vraight*, i. e. the chief head of a clan, or principal
" Chieftain, from *Ard*, high, and *Vracht*, a fupport; or
" *Vraight*, a potentate; the Chieftains of the *Irifh* Septs
" being ftill to this day called *Vraights*, as Camden tells
" us in *Brit.* IRELAND, COLERANE. See Lhuyd's Ar-
" chæol. Brit. in Irifh-Englifh Dictionary." To this imaginary Arviragus, the filver coin in Camden I. 25. with an
armed head and ARIVOG on the obv. and horfe galloping
with ONONVS on the reverfe, is afcribed both by Speed (4),
and Abp. Ufher (5); that gold coin alfo in Camd. I. 27.
without a legend, Speed feems to think may be the pro-

(1) Baxt. Gl. voc. ARVIRAGUS, CARATACUS, and CUNOBELINUS.
(2) Wife, p. 226.
(3) Gent. Magaz. 1757. p. 59.
(4) Speed, Hift. p. 35.
(5) Ufher, Brit. Eccl. Antiq. p. 12, 288.

perty

COINS OF CUNOBELIN. 59

perty of the same Prince (1); but Ob. Walker (2) esteems it a groundless conjecture, as I dare say your Lordship will: And as to the former of these coins, Mr. Wise observes, " Integrior nummus Pembrokianus legit ARIVOS " SANTONOS ; qui forte ad *Santones* Galliæ Aquitaniæ " populum spectat. Quod si ARIVOS *Ariovistum*, a Cæsare " devictum, legant alii, ipse non refragabor (3)." This, doubtless, is a plausible conjecture; however, we may be very certain, Arviragus, if ever there were such a person, has no title to this coin.

I am next to mention a silver coin of Bericus (4), who was contemporary with Caratacus and Togodumnus, as likewise with their father Cunobelin. The account we have of this penny, is this: Mr. Ed. Lhuyd, in his famous preface to his countrymen, prefixed to the Archæologia (5), says, " As to the Britains, we can easily prove " (for it is plain demonstration) that they had letters be- " fore the time of Juvenal and Tacitus; for I have lately " seen a coin of *Berach*, or Bericus, with his name upon " it, in the time of the Emperor Claudius, &c." It appears to me, that Mr. Lhuyd had communicated this coin to Mr. Baxter, with whom he corresponded; for he, in his Glossary, p. 58. gives a more particular account of it, " Hujus *Berici* argenteum nummum vidisse se testatur

---

(1) Speed, Hist. p. 73.
(2) See him in Camden.
(3) Wise, p. 227.
(4) Dio, p. 779. Mr. Baxt. in Gloss. p. 58. calls him Caius Bericus; but I believe upon no authority, and esteems him to have been of the rank of a *Regulus*, or petty King.
(5) This was written in the British tongue, but is translated into English by himself and others, in Lewis's Hist. of Britain, p. 59. seq.

" Luidius

"Luidius noster in Archæologia, cujus capiti circum-
"scribebatur BIRIC: & in aversâ parte porci erat sig-
"num." This coin certainly bids fair to be a genuine
coin of Bericus; but then, as Mr. Baxter observes (1),
"Verum oportuit Percussorem hujus nummi fuisse Ro-
"manum." *It must have been Roman work*, and for
what we can tell, might have been the production of
Tascio himself; however, every thing that respects it is
perfectly consistent with what we have delivered above.

I esteem it probable, that when once Tascio had begun to stamp money for Cunobelin, the Britons themselves would be trying, in imitation of him, to strike
money; and from their hand might come some of those
rough and barbarous pieces, that are really British; nay,
some of them, for ought we know, may be coins of Cunobelin, tho' they cannot be appropriated to him with
any certainty, for want of the necessary data. But there
were *Reguli* in the island, independent of Cunobelin, and
others of these concave shapeless pennies may appertain
to them; and when the Romans left the country, and
either carried away or concealed a good part of their
specie, the British Pendragons would necessarily be obliged
to make some mean essays; and afterwards, when the
Britons were driven into Wales and Cornwall by the
Saxons, they would be necessitated to attempt something
in the pecuniary way in those parts. These suppositions,
all taken together, sufficiently account, we think, for the
great number of the British pennies found here, as also for
the rudeness of the workmanship in them; and lastly,
for the difficulty of ascribing them to their true and pro-

(1) Letters prefixed to Baxt. Gloss.

per Princes; these coins wanting, in general, both letters, and all other necessary marks for the doing of this.

I make here one general, and very material observation, that whether I am right or wrong in the interpretation of the word TASCIA, the rest of this epistle will not be affected by it, since the coins will, nevertheless, all of them appertain to Cunobelin. This Prince will still be connected with TASCIO, whatever is the sense and meaning of the word; and consequently the business of appropriation, as above and in the sequel, the commentary upon these coins, and the demonstration of the several uses to be made of them, will all stand upon a firm and solid bottom, let what will become of our conjecture.

Now, my Lord, that I have done with this long enquiry about TASCIO, I must add a few words, and but a few; for I shall make your Lordship amends here, by way of appropriating the coins of the 3d and 4th classes. The King's name appears at length on many of these coins, in conjunction with that of Tascio; whence it seems but reasonable, that where only CVN or CVNO is seen with TASCIO, Cunobelin must be meant, and nobody else. And the case will be the same, if there be only a part of the word TASCIO; for such initials, when connected and joined with CVNOBELIN, or a part of his name, cannot in reason stand for any thing else but the word TASCIO, which we see written in other cases so plainly at full length. The fourth class stands exactly upon the same bottom.

To come then to the 5th and 6th classes: TASCIO in the 5th class stands alone; but then he was plainly connected with CVNOBELIN, as appears from the 3d and 4th classes, and, as we think, was a mint-master of his: For whom therefore

therefore could these coins be made but for him? However, I desire it may be further considered, that Cunobelin lived in all appearance to a great age, being alive in Caligula's time; so that Tascio, who could not be a young man, weighing all circumstances, when he first came into his service, cannot in reason be thought to have served any other master; being a man so eminent in his business, as to be fetched into Britain for the purpose of introducing the new art of coining, of practising it, and instructing the Britons therein, we cannot well judge him inferior in years to Cunobelin himself, but rather to be older, and probably much older of the two. I add, it has been above hinted, that Cunobelin's sons struck no money at all; and it would be highly unreasonable to imagine, Tascio should coin for any other family but his. These coins consequently must be all of them Cunobelin's: In short, the coins are plainly the work of Tascio, for his name, or a part of it, appears upon them; and for that reason, we think, reflecting on the connexion between him and Cunobelin, they ought in all reason to be esteemed his. But to drive this nail up to the head, you will please to observe, that TASCIO, on the first coin of the 6th class, is joined with VER, or Verulam, as it ought to be interpreted, a city or town of Cunobelin's, shewing clearly that the coin is his, tho' his name be not expressed upon it: Insomuch, that Tascio was not only connected with him, as appears from the 3d and 4th classes, but actually wrought at his city, as appears from this coin. The arguments respecting the 6th class run also in the same manner; this and the former class confirming one another, and with the light they receive from the 3d and 4th class, clafs, afcertaining themfelves with fufficient clearnefs to this Prince; wherefore, as the fecond coin in this clafs has the word CEARATIC upon it, we take it to be the name of a place, and can put no other fenfe upon it; it muft neceffarily, we think, be fome confiderable city or town within Cunobelin's dominions, but at this day unknown. The confequence is, it cannot be a coin of Caratacus.

I go now, my Lord, on the commentary or defcription I fpoke of, which I propofe to contract as much as pof- fible, having already premifed a wifh, that the Speedian and the Camdenian coins were more minutely re-infpected, and feveral particulars more fully examined, which I fhall not need to repeat, but only refer to.

CLASS

CLASS I.

No. 1.

THIS is a very elegant coin in silver, and represents, I think, the King's head, à la Romaine, without any ornament. The name, which is written at length, is particular, having I instead of E in the third syllable, which is not to be wondered at, since the orthography of the antient British language must have been at that time in a very fluctuating and unsettled state. It is written in the same manner on class III. no. 1, 4, 8, and 10. The truth, however, I presume, is CVNOBELIN, as being most agreeable to the etymology. The reverse of this coin presents us with a noble horse, and over him a crescent.

No. 2.

The King's name, CVN, occurs here on both sides, which is remarkable; and yet we see an instance of the same kind, in the coin of TOCIRIX, in Lord Pembr. Part II. pl. 93. no. 10. I suspect the same in the next coin in that plate; and see below, class V. no. 5. It appears to be the same coin that is engraved in Lord Pembroke's collection, Part II. pl. 94. no. 5. only there it is copper, whereas it is silver here. The figure, which is at full length and walking, is naked, but has a cap or helmet. And as the club on his shoulder is knotted in Lord Pembroke's type, I have declared my opinion above, in fa-

COINS OF CUNOBELIN. 65

vour of Hercules. Mr. Walker indeed esteems it the portrait of an ordinary foot soldier, with a head-piece and armour down to his thighs, and club upon his shoulder, not considering that the common soldiers of the Britons, at this time, had no defensive armour. See Dio Nicæus, Herodian, and Mr. Walker himself, in Camd. col. CXXI.

No. 3.

See the coin last described.

No. 4.

It is very difficult to determine what the animal on the obv. of this copper coin may be: Mr. Wise calls it a horse; but it is more like a sheep or a dog, either of which is, undoubtedly, a proper device for a British coin; their dogs being famous, and the sheep a most useful creature to them, both for its milk and wool, as will be shewn hereafter. It seems there were some letters on this coin, tho' now effaced: This obliges us to register the coin here, tho' it would otherwise belong to a different assortment.

No. 5.

For want of the rev. I am forced to register this coin from Mr. Selden's Titles of honour, Part I. ch. 8. in this place; it would otherwise probably fall into another class. The author has also omitted the metal, but what he writes upon it is this: " It seems by the old British " monies, that the diadem or fillet, perhaps, of Pearl " also, was worne by King Cunobelin; one kind of them " was of this forme."

CLASS II.

No. 1.

THE type of this brafs coin, which is alfo given us by Alford, we think, reprefents Janus, and that CAMV means Camulodunum, the place of coinage. See what has been faid already on both thefe points. There is a fimilar coin of Lord Pembroke's, Part II. pl. 94. no. 6. where the animal is evidently a hog, but the tree is wanting. Trees appear on Mr. Borlafe's coins, no. 2, 3, 6. The infcription in Lord Pembroke is more perfect, CAMVL. All I fhall note further is, That in Lord Pemb. Plate 95. no. 5. the head of Janus likewife appears, on a filver coin, with a horfe and rider on the reverfe, as on that piece of Cunobelin, in our 6th clafs, no. 2. and therefore may poffibly be his.

No. 2. and 4.

Thefe are both gold (1). The firft has a horfe, with a wheel, or perhaps the fun, under him, and a comet over him; and on the obv. CAMV, with an ear of corn. The wheel is abfent from the fecond; the o in CVNO is alfo differently placed, and the thing over the horfe feems to be either a leaf or an ear of corn. The fecond of thefe coins is engraved in Battely's Antiq. Rutup. p. 93. where the o is evidently a crefcent, and there is a jagged leaf, or a branch over the horfe. *A*.

---

(1) The fecond is marked wrong in Camden.

COINS OF CUNOBELIN.

No. 3.

This silver coin, from Speed, has a Victory sitting on a chair. There is a Victory also on a British unknown coin in Camd. tab. I. 12. The obv. presents us with the King's head, with the hair uncurl'd, and kept upright by means of a fillet or diadem placed at the origine of the hair.

No. 5.

This is gold, and on the obv. has a spica, or ear of corn, with MCV, which I esteem, as also Walker does, to indicate the place of coinage. The rev. has a horse, with CVN.

No. 6.

This brass coin has two figures standing upon the obv. with CVN. The foremost, which is naked all but about the loins, seems to be Cunobelin stretching out something which he holds in his hand; and the other, which seems to turn its back towards us, out of modesty as it were, very probably is his Queen. The rev. has a Pegasus, with CAMV.

No. 7.

For this brass piece, see no. I. of this class.

No. 8.

This is gold. A horſe curvetting, under him the ſun with CVN, and over him a ſtar of ſix rays, with what perhaps may be an imperfect creſcent. The rev. has an ear of corn, with CAMV.

Camd. col. CCCCXVI.

" Upon an old coin of Cunobeline . : . . I have ſeen a
" figure with a helmet and a ſpear, which probably was
" that of Mars; with the letters CAMV." This alſo ſeems to have been the opinion of Alford, p. 6. But ſurely one has more reaſon to think it Cunobelin himſelf.

Camd. col. CXII.

" I have likewiſe ſeen another [coin] with Pegaſus
" and CAMV; and on the rev. a man's head, with an
" helmet and a ſhield between ears of Corn and
" CVNO."

CLASS III.

No. 1.

THE King's head on this brass coin seems to have a cap of some sort upon it, and differs in that from the 3d of the second class, where the hair is so visible. I look upon it to be a regal ornament, the common people wearing their hair long, as will be shewn hereafter. This is a very remarkable coin, on account of the rev. on which, in Camden's type, the mint-master is sitting at work, which is evidently that of coining money, there being several pieces just dropped, as it were, from under the hammer. The same coin occurs in Lord Pembr. only the falling pieces are there wanting, as likewise they are on Mr. Duane's coin, no. 2. in Dr. Pettingal, which entirely resembles Lord Pembroke's, except that Mr. Duane's has CVNOBELIN, and not CVNOBILIN. Quære, if one of the coins be not misrepresented? The British money, it seems, was struck by a sort of hammer; the reverse being cut on a die, placed underneath the piece of metal that was to be struck.

No. 2.

The Laureate crown on the obv. and the Pegasus on the rev. of this silver coin, have been already considered.

No. 3.

Mr. Walker takes the obv. to be a woman's head; if so, it may be Cunobelin's Queen, he being a married man; but if he only judged from the absence of the beard, this particular will not bear him out, Cæsar informing us, that the Britons shaved their hair every where, except on the head and the upper lip. De B. G. V. c. 14. 'tis more probably Cunobelin himself. The Sphinx on the rev. of this silver piece has been before noticed.

No. 4.

The metal of this is not expressed, but the obv. has a horse, with an imperfect crescent over him; and the rev. the King's head, with his hair, but without the fillet or diadem, as in the 3d of the second class. Authors are not always exact in the matter of obverse and reverse; but I chuse to follow them, for the avoiding of confusion, tho' I think them sometimes wrong; as in this case, where the obv. evidently stands in the place of the rev. and *vice versâ*.

No. 5.

This elegant copper coin of Mr. Duane's is very remarkable; the King's head on the obv. is much à la Romaine, and the name is not only latinized CVNOBELINVS, but we have also RE upon it as part of his title REX, particulars evidently bespeaking it to be the performance of a Roman

COINS OF CUNOBELIN.

a Roman master, as has been already noted. The rev. presents us with a bull or cow, the like animal also appearing, but in a different posture, and as pushing with the horns, on the 1st of class V.

No. 6.

The Queen's head, for her's I take it to be, with the hair. As for the other particulars relative to this copper piece, see the description of no. 1. in this class.

No. 7.

There is a most excellent Sphinx on this curious silver coin, which is totally different from no. 3. in this class. The head, I suppose, is of the feminine kind, as representing the goddess Victory, concerning whom see before.

No. 8.

The King's head, à la Romaine, appears on this silver coin, which is inscribed CVNOBILIN. Over the horse on the rev. there is a part of a circle; perhaps it was intended for a crescent, corresponding in that respect also with no. 1. class I.

No. 9.

This brass coin, which has CVNOBILIN, with the King's head on the obv. and the mint-master sitting at work on the

the rev. has been confidered before; fee no. 1. of this clafs.

No. 10.

This coin, which is of the fame metal, exhibits the King's head à la Romaine, and laureated, which is very extraordinary, with the infcription CVNOBILIN. The rev. has a horfe ftanding ftill; and the legend, which is very faint, feems to give us the word TASCIA.

CLASS IV.

No. 1.

THE coins of this clafs are the moft perfect and complete of any, as to the legend. This filver one, which is engraved alfo in Alford, has the King's buft clothed, with the hair dreffed clofe to the head. Mr. Camden, Alford, and the authors of the Univ. Hift. vol. XIX. p. 130. efteem it, but I know not for what reafon, a woman's head, the two latter thinking it to reprefent Britain. The rev. has Apollo fitting and playing on his harp, exactly like no. 3. in this clafs. Walker calls the rev. a hog and wolf incorporated, a note which I fuppofe is put in that place by miftake, fince in all probability it belongs to Camden I. 14. where fee this author. The infcription on the obv. is TASCNOVANE; and Walker thinks Novanci may denote fome unknown city in the dominions of Cunobelin;

Cunobelin; but others incline to interpret it, the tribute of the Novantes (1). This is probable enough, as Mr. Duane's coin, no. 5. in this clafs, has plainly TASC NOVA; the perfect word, I suppose, would be NOVANETUM, the E being inserted, as presently we shall see the I is in a similar case. Dr. Pettingal thinks the people of the province were called *Novantes*, and he vouches this coin (2), whilst the inhabitants of the city were called *Trinobantes*, from *Tre*, a town or city; so that *Trinobantes* signified *the city of the Novantes* (3). This is very plausible, and yet there lies an objection against it, since Cæsar, lib. V. mentions the Trinobantes as a nation. I know not how to get over this: However, there is a third coin in this clafs, viz. no. 2. where the inscription runs TASCIIOVANIT, and where 'tis possible, especially as this coin comes to us by Mr. Speed, the II may be N, and then it will imply TASC NOVANITVM, as here, I being inserted instead of E.

No. 2.

This silver coin has the King's bust in armour, with a good helmet. The rev. has a hog, with very long pricked ears, see no. 1. in clafs II. The inscription on the rev. has been just now considered.

(1) So Dr. Pettingal, p. 5. and Alford. " Obscurior vox illa NOVANE; " Nisi forte Nouantum, vel Trinobantum urbem, Britanniæ principem, velis " accipere," p. 4. And so Baxter, p. 184, 231. " in Britannico quodam " nummulo etiam NOVANEI, sive potius NOVANTI, legitur pro Trinovantes."
(2) See also Univ. Hist. XIX. p. 130.
(3) See also Mr. Baxter, p. 230.

No. 3.

The King's head on this silver coin has a cap on, not greatly unlike the 1st in clafs III. Walker talks of it being the head of a city. Apollo playing on the rev. has been before noticed. This coin is evidently the production of the fame hand as no. 1. in this clafs, and the infcription TASC VANIT, feems to import it was coined at one of the Ventæ, perhaps at Venta Silurum, fince we find Caratacus, the fon of Cunobelin, figuring at the head of this nation; or, if Mr. Baxter be right in thinking Cunobelin was King of the Iceni, at Venta Icenorum (1), the word at length would be VANITAE, where A is for E, and I is inferted, as we have feen it before. Quære, whether, as this coin fo much refembles no. 1. of this clafs, that word be not mifdivided and mifread, and we ought not to read, TASCIO VANE, for TASC NOVANE, as it is given above. This fuppofition will not exclude the Novantes from our coins, becaufe Mr. Duane's coin, the 5th in this clafs, fo plainly has TASC NOVA. Walker is fo abfurd as to think VANIT the fame as VANOC, in Camden I. 14.

(1) Horfeley, p. 17. feems to think Caffivellaun was monarch of the Iceni; if fo, Cunobelin probably alfo was. See him again, p. 31, 34. Thus Mr. Baxter, in regard of Cunobelin, " Crediderim etiam Icenorum " fuiffe Regem, adeoque Brigantici generis, quod Caratacum filium præ" fecerit Siluribus, et Togodumnum (uti ex nomine conjicio) Dobunis.... ". Quinetiam, autore Dione, Camalodunum regui ejus caput fuerat; quod " cum in finibus Icenimagnorum fuerit, illorum juris initio fuiffe cenfendum " eft, cum in Ptolemæo fit Trinoüantum." So again, p. 67. he calls Cunobelin King of the *Uigantes* or *Iceni*. And fee him, p. 64, 70, 137.

No.

No. 4.

This copper coin reprefents plainly the King's head à la Romaine, and on the rev. a Centaur. The infcription has been already remarked.

No. 5.

On this filver piece there is a very fine Hercules, as has been before mentioned. The rev. gives a woman riding fideways on an animal, but uncertain what; for it does not feem to be Europa's bull, nor Cybele's lion. Cybele was both a Gaulifh deity (1), and a Britifh one, according to Richard of Cirencefter, p. 9. But this creature has more the appearance of a dog; and Mr. Thorefby fpeaks of a dog on a coin of his, Mufeum, p. 338. The infcription TASC NOVA has been above confidered.

CLASS V.

No. 1.

THIS is a very capital coin in filver, fuppofed, and with great reafon, to reprefent the head of Auguftus Cæfar, with TASCIA, which perhaps may be the true orthography of the name on the obv. and on the rev. a

(1) Montf. II. p. 279.

fine bull, pushing with his horns, intended perhaps for the sign Taurus, as in that coin of Augustus, Lord Pembr. III. pl. 94. The laureate diadem, after this time, seems to have grown common in Britain; for which see Mr. Borlase, p. 244, bis, 245, sæpe, and p. 246, bis; and quære, whether that strange piece of work on the coin which Dr. Plott took to be Prasutagus and Boadicea, may not have been designed for something of this kind.

No. 2.

A gold coin of Mr. Speed's, with Cunobelin on horse-back, and the inscription TASCO on the obverse. This, Mr. Speed, as has been remarked, ascribes to Cassivel-laun, but on no good grounds (1). It is not certainly known, what the device on the rev. of this coin is, but it seems to be a flower, see Walker in Camden col. CXI. and yet Mr. Borlase, p. 243. speaks of two dolphins turn-ing their crooked backs to each other, of which I can discern no manner of resemblance.

No. 3.

This piece was fully considered along with the last.

No. 4.

This, which is silver, has a horse, with a shield in the form of a lozenge, hanging on his side, on the oby. and only the letters TASC in a compartment on the rev. 'Tis

(1) See above pag. 35, 36.

a doubt

a doubt with me, whether it be a stone horse, or whether it be not mounted by a rider imperfectly expressed.

No. 5.

This coin is of electrum, and has a horse on the gallop, with TASC on the obv. and on the rev. TASCIO, or TASCI. As for the sameness of the legend on both sides, see above, class I. no. 2.

Thoresby in Muf. p. 338.

" This is the largest of silver, and very fair: On the
" convex side a head well performed; in the concave a
" dog and TA, the initials of TASCIA or tribute money,
" under a man on horseback."

CLASS VI.

No. 1.

THIS silver coin, we suppose, was struck at Verulam, and so does Mr. Horseley (1), and W. Vallans (2). There is a good horse galloping on the rev. with the name, and, as I think, correctly written, TASCIA. Mr. Camd. col. CXIII. by mistake, reads VERV, and Vallans

(1) P. 15. where, as also p. 30, see much about this place.
(2) Vallans in Lel. Itin. V. p. xv.

more

more corruptly TASC. VERVL. Mr. Wife interprets it, "Vernemetum, or Verbinum, or Veronum, of Gallia Belgica," acknowledging that our people explain it of Verulam, as indeed all in general do. The coin is engraved by Mr. Hearne, in Lel. Itin. V. p. v.

No. 2.

Cunobelin is mounted on this gold coin, in a fighting posture, with his sword (1) and shield, on a galloping horse; and the inscription is CEARATIC, which we imagine to be the name of some town in his territory, tho' at present unknown. Camden guesses it to be a coin of the warlike Caratacus; and certainly, if Caratacus, or Caractacus, coined any money, this piece may be thought to have some pretension to him. "Ego autem," says Mr. Wife, "ad Carretanos Vasconum Hispaniæ gentem referre malim." Walker observes, that some read it EPATICA, which, says he, may keep its native signification, since we find parsley, the palm, vine, myrtle, cynoglossum, laserpitium, and other plants, sometimes figured, sometimes only named, upon coins; as you may see in Spanhemius. I differ, however, from all these authors, on account of the rev. which has an ear of corn, with a corrupt inscription TASCIE; a clear evidence with me, that the true owner of the piece is Cunobelin, the patron and friend of Tascia.

AFTER finishing this short description of the coins, we will try, my Lord, if you please, what instruction, or mat-

---

(1) Camden calls it a spear.

COINS OF CUNOBELIN. 79

ters of erudition, this curious cabinet will afford us; how far they may serve to illustrate the antiquities of our country, or contribute to confirm those few notices, which the antients have left us concerning it.

I shall begin with the Prince himself: His life was prolonged to a great age, since he flourished in the reigns of Augustus, Tiberius, and Caligula, whose power he revered, and whose friendship he cultivated. The intercourse between the Romans and Britons, in his time, was frequent and considerable, much greater than commonly imagined; and extremely beneficial it proved to his subjects, as may appear in the sequel. He seems to have been of a very martial disposition; for tho' he chose, upon prudence, to live in amity and good harmony with the Romans, whose imposts were moderate, yet we see him in armour upon the coins: There also we see Hercules, Victory, his own head laureate (1); and on one piece, according to the opinion of Mr. Camden, the God Mars (2). However, his veneration for this deity is abundantly conspicuous from the name he imposed on his metropolis, Camulodunum, importing its consecration to Camulus, the Celtic, or British, name of the God of War. There is reason to believe he was engaged in almost continual wars with the neighbouring states in the island, and therein was very successful (3); insomuch, that the goddess of Victory appears with propriety upon his money.

(1) Class III. no. 10.
(2) See the 2d class.
(3) See what will be said below of his dominions, and the enlargement of them, by himself.

Cunobelin's

Cunobelin's devotion was little lefs to the Roman mufical deity Apollo, as appears from the coins, to which in this part of the effay my defign is chiefly to confine myfelf. He bore the name, as has been obferved, of this deity, according to the notion and idea the Britons entertained of him; a circumftance which would infallibly difpofe him, as foon as he was informed of the conformity or identity of the Latin and Auguftaen Apollo, to communicate and extend his adorations unto him. Auguftus had an efpecial regard for this deity, and Cunobelin omitted no opportunity of making his court to that Emperor; hence came his effigies, and the Sphinx, upon the coins that iffued from his mints: But Cunobelin's veneration for Apollo, or Belinus, we may have occafion to touch upon again hereafter.

Our Prince was not only warlike, but alfo great and powerful; his family was flourifhing, and his dominions extenfive; three of his fons have been already mentioned, but it appears from Tacitus he had feveral more; the brothers of Caratacus (tho' Togodumnus was then dead, and it is not known what was become of Adminius) being taken captives along with him, and carried to Rome (1). His Queen appears, as we think, upon his coins, clafs II. no. 6. clafs III. no. 6. (2); and Mr. Baxter, who loves to indulge in conjectures (in which he is fagacious, but often not a little vifionary), is of opinion, he was the hufband of Cartifmandua, Queen of the Brigantes (3), fhe being his fecond wife, and furviving him (4).

(1) Tacitus Annal. XII. c. 35, 37.
(2) That in clafs III. no. 3. perhaps may be doubtful.
(3) Baxter, Gloff. voc. CUNOBELINUS.
(4) Carte, p. 110. and Baxter, Gloff. p. 67, 70, 137.

As

As to the other point I mentioned, to wit, his dominions, " Cunobelin, Prince of the Cattuvellauni, who
" had, since Julius Cæsar's time, to use the words of
" Mr. Carte, extended their territories so, as to bring the
" Trinovantes (among whom Ptolemy places Camulo-
" dunum) the Dobuni, and other clans of people under
" their vassalage, was, by this accession of dominion, the
" most powerful Prince in the island (1)." This author observes, he made his son Togodumnus, Governor of the Dobuni, as his name imports (2). That Caratacus " pro-
" bably presided over those quarters of the country of
" the Cattuvellauni, that lay next the Silures, and pos-
" sessed them in property after his father's death; if he
" did not, by the exclusion of Adminius the eldest of
" the brothers, succeed him in all his other dominions.
" Adminius seems, in Cunobelin's life-time, to have pre-
" sided over the Trinovantes (3)." The same author, in another place, remarks, that the territories of Cattuvellauni " now reached from Lincolnshire eastward, thro'
" the shires of Northampton and Worcester, to the banks
" of the Severn westward.—Bedford and Hertfordshire,
" and the western part of Middlesex, were their antient
" possessions; which they had much enlarged by con-
" quests over the Belgic Britains, that lay contiguous to
" them; having, in Cunobelin's time, reduced the Tri-
" novantes (who inhabited the rest of Middlesex, and a
" great part of Essex) the Ancalites, and part of the Do-

(1) Carte, p. 98.
(2) Carte, p. 98. and 100. Also Baxter, Gloss. in voc. DOBUNI, CUNOBELINUS, TOGODUMNUS, ICENI. Dio, p. 779.
(3) Carte, ibid.

" buni

"buni settled; the one in the hills of Bucks and Oxford-
"shire, near Henley, the other in the vale of Aylesbury,
"and the lower part of the latter county (1)." Perhaps
the author may not be precisely right in all this (2); but
his opinion, that the territories of Cunobelin were large,
is undoubtedly true. Mr. Baxter, who esteems Cunobelin to have been the Ardirag or Pendragon of the whole
island (3), thinks he had invested his son Caratacus with
the government over the Silures (4). The places mentioned in the coins, are Camulodonum in Essex, Verulam
in Hertfordshire, Venta Silurum, or Icenorum, Cearatic
and *w* cv, two places which yet want to be investigated,
in which I should be glad of your Lordship's assistance (5).

But leaving this martial and politic Prince, for such
we may justly stile him, in regard of his artful and pru-
dent conduct towards the Romans, throughout the whole
extent of his long reign, we will now turn to something
else. And here we may observe, in the first place, how
early the theology of Pagan Rome began to creep into this
island. We have upon this one set of coins, Janus, the
musical Apollo, Victory, Hercules, Pegasus, the Sphinx,
and the Centaur. The original British deities, we are
told, were of most shapeless and horrible forms (6), without any thing amiable or inviting in them; and such, I

---

(1) Carte, p. 100.
(2) Compare Horseley, p. 33. seq.
(3) Baxt. Gl. voc. CUNOBELINUS, CARATACUS, ICENI.
(4) ——— voc. CARATACUS, TOGODUMNUS, ICENI.
(5) Quære, Whether the first may not mean Chertsey?
(6) So Gildas, " Nec enumerans patriæ portenta ipsa diabolica, pene
" numero vincentia Ægyptiaca (quorum nonnulla, lineamentis adhuc de-
" formibus intra vel extra deserta mœnia, solito more rigentia torvis vulti-
" bus intuemur) neque, &c." p. 12.

presume,

presume, was the goddess Andrasta, and probably Cunobelin's own Camulus, as also Mars Braciaca (1), and Cernunnos (2); but these new figures presented them with something of a more gentle kind, and more pleasing to the eye; and no doubt the agreeableness of their portraits contributed greatly to facilitate their reception. We may depend upon it, that the rites and ceremonies attendant on the worship of these heathen deities, all entered the country along with them; insomuch, that in Cunobelin's reign, and very principally by the means of Tascio, his learned and skilful artist, the Britons were instructed very amply, both in the old Greek and Roman theology, and in the various and accustomed modes of their worship.

The Roman letters also, the elements of their learning, were introduced at the same time with their religion. This now was in truth a most noble and useful acquisition, and in all appearance accompanied the person of Tascio; and if the natives of this island did not enjoy, till his arrival, the use and benefit of alphabetical letters, as some have thought, the blessing was inestimably great: However, we may reasonably suppose, that the Roman letters did not arrive singly, but were attended, as with a natural effect, with some portions of their knowledge, some glimmerings of the Roman arts and sciences. The use of coined money was evidently, upon our hypothesis, imported at this juncture, together with the art of making and striking it. This certainly was an unspeakable advantage in conducting the little trade they had; for though, as has been alledged, traffic and commerce may

(1) See above.
(2) Montf. II. p. 271.

be carried on in a crude and superficial manner, even without money, and rather better by pieces of metal, rings, or tallies, adjusted to a certain weight; yet a stamp or impression upon the pieces, when generally known and approved, must be allowed as to have vastly the preference, so to expedite, to shorten and promote the grand affair of commerce in all shapes. In short, the art the Britons became possessed of by Tascio's means, was so beneficial in its nature to them, that they were not permitted, by those who were afterwards their masters, to practise it for any long continuance (1).

The British coins found at Karn Brè, are said to be of pure gold; and Mr. Thoresby speaks of some of pure silver, of good brass and copper, or of iron (2); but in general the coins of Cunobelin are far from being of a fine texture, whether gold, or silver, or brass; from whence it may seem plain, that the Britons learnt the art, at this time, of mixing and alloying their metals to advantage; an invention, which, whatever might become of the art of coining amongst them, could not fail of being extremely serviceable to them in other respects, in the fabrication both of their utensils and arms. However, it must not be dissembled, in this place, that Dr. Plott (3) thinks the electrum, used by the Britons, was of the native, and not of the factitious kind, because the matter of the coins is not of an equal or uniform mixture, but some of it is richer in gold than other. But, for my part, I find no

(1) See what has been said above, on the stop which the Romans put to the British mints.
(2) Thoresby, Muf. p. 337.
(3) See also Thoresby, l. c. This author doubts, however, p. 338.

instance

instance of a native electrum ever found here; and therefore so long as the art of compounding metals might be taught the Britons by the Romans, there is no need to have recourse to an exotic mineral. The variety, or the fluctuating proportions of the allay, is no conclusive argument in favour of a native electrum being used, since such variation might just as well happen in a compound made by art. The silver of the coins, moreover, is as much allayed as the gold (1); wherefore as the Britons, or Tascio for them, debased this metal so much, is it not exceeding probable they did the same by the other? Nay, one cannot imagine the Britons should be able to make brass, without their understanding more of the metallurgic art than these authors seem to suppose. The celts, as they are called, which with Mr. Hearne's leave (2) are British, and not Roman implements, as has been lately shewn by an able hand (3), are evidently of brass, being a composition of copper and tin, or lead (4); that is, as Dr. Richardson asserts, of two parts of coarse copper, and one of lead (5).

But the Roman customs and manners in general seem to have gained a footing here in this reign. Cunobelin appears in armour, and Apollo is playing upon his harp. The first indicating the beginning, probably, of the use of defensive armour, and the other the introduction of the Roman lyre. For though, amongst the several articles of the druidical superstition, and their personal qualifica-

(1) Wise, p. 227.
(2) Hearne, in Lel. Itin. I. p. 117. seq.
(3) Borlase, p. 263.
(4) Borlase, p. 267, 271, 272.
(5) Richardson, in Lel. Itin. I. p. 141.

tions and accomplishments, we hear of their musical skill; yet their performances, we may imagine, were but rude and inharmonious, compared with the execution of Greece and Rome: Music, one has reason to think, received great improvement in Britain at this juncture, and consequently that the Welsh and Irish harps, but ill-shapen before, were from thenceforward modelled more after the Apollinarian or Roman manner.

These, we will suppose, were but slender commencements; but, however, they laid the foundation of those vast advancements and improvements, which afterwards ensued, when the nation had so far adopted and cultivated the Roman manners, as to be noticed for it by the historians (1); and, as Gildas testifies, to deserve to be called the *Roman island.* Mr. Walker is of opinion, and one cannot help joining with him, that the ingress and admission of the Roman manners and customs into the island, so greatly tending to soften and meliorate the natural ferocity of the inhabitants, contributed mightily to facilitate the reception of the Christian religion (2) soon after. Insomuch, that the first invasion of the island by Julius Cæsar, the correspondence afterwards maintained with the Romans by Cunobelin, and the progress of the imperial arms in the reign of Claudius, seem to have been permitted and directed by an all-wise providence, for the salutary purpose of civilizing and converting this heathen nation, from the grossness of error and superstition, to the truth and purity of the Christian faith (3).

(1) Tacitus, Vit. Agric. c. 21. Pettingal, p. 6. Walker, in Camd. col. CXVII.
(2) Walker, ibid.
(3) Alford, p. 2.

COINS OF CUNOBELIN. 87

To turn back for a moment to affairs of science. The Druids, or at least one order of them, as we are told by the antients (1), was deeply engaged in physiology, or the study of natural things; and, amongst other branches of the subject, did not neglect the phænomena of the heavens. The moon, when six days old, was very principally regarded by them, the misletoe being cut, " Sexta " Luna, quæ, says Pliny, principia mensium annorum- " que his facit, et seculi post tricesimum annum, quia " jam virium abunde habeat, nec sit sui dimidia (2)." The crescent was consequently in great vogue with them (3); as also the moon was at other ages (4).

But allowing the Druids to have been already possessed of some useful astronomical observations, their stock of knowledge this way was undoubtedly much increased by the accession of that superior skill, which the Greeks and Romans therein had. For tho' the Greeks were reckoned to excel the Romans in this science at first (5), the Romans by this time had naturalized all their learning. Sun, moon, stars and comets, all make their appearance on the coins; and some small sparks of science, relative to them, would of course attend them; more, I mean, than what they could boast of before: For how highly soever the skill and knowledge of the Druids, in these celestial matters, may by certain authors have been extolled, one has no reason to think they exceeded the Romans therein,

(1) Amm. Marcel. XV. c. 9. Cæsar, de B. G. VI. c. 14. Strabo IV. p. 197. Cic. de Divin. I. c. 41.
(2) Plin. N. H. XVI. c. 44.
(3) See below; as also Montf. tom. II. p. 278. on Plate LXI. no. 2.
(4) Plin. XXIX. c. 3. unless the same sixth day be there meant.
(5) Virg. Æn. VI. 848.

but

but rather must have been vastly inferior to them. But this affair of the stars and crescents will be resumed hereafter.

At present, let us see in what manner these remains of Cunobelin's reign may assist in corroborating the accounts given us of the manners of the antient Britons, by the historians; and how far the coins, and the written monuments, mutually conspire to illustrate and confirm one another. This, I presume, is one material use to be made of the coins of any antient nation whatsoever.

That the Britons had gold within themselves, has been noted above; and both Strabo and Tacitus inform us, they had silver; and they are well supported by the metal of many of the coins, which consist of those materials, tho' often debased.

We here see the swine (1); and the connexion between the wild boar and the forest, is in a manner natural. Thus Arabia, for want of woodlands, produces no hogs (2); and the old provincial saying, concerning the county of Nottingham, ran, on account of its vast forest,

" Notynghamshire ful of hogges (3)."

And as the Britons subsisted so much upon flesh, refusing even to taste fish (4), and having no corn in the interior of the island, this animal must have been in the highest request, as also it was among the Belgæ of Gaul (5).

(1) See also the account of Bericus's coin above, and Pliny, Lib. XXIV. c. 11.
(2) Mr. Sale's Prelim. Diss. to the Koran, p. 170.
(3) Lel. Itin. V. p. xxvi.
(4) Xiphilinus.
(5) Strabo IV. p. 197.

And

And no doubt, but as hunting is particularly noted by Xiphilinus (1), as an exercise to which they were much addicted, this beast was certainly one principal object of it. The wilds and forests of Britain were immense, at the time the Romans first came hither; there were no less than three vast Caledonian woods (2), to take no notice of others (3). In one coin the hog stands besides a tree, and trees are not unfrequently represented on the Karn Brê coins. These trees were probably the oak, held in such profound veneration here, on account of the tree itself, the grove it formed, and the misletoe it produced (4); and not a little, I conceive, in respect of the acorn, the best and most fattening food, in a state of nature, for the animal in question. More therefore is signified by the boar on the coins, than Mr. Walker suggests, viz. that he was an emblem of strength; and indeed, were this all, it would not so well accord with a sow and pigs in one of the British coins (5). The beech, 'tis true, affords a good mast; but Cæsar tells us Britain was then without this tree, " Materia cujusque " generis, ut in Gallia est, præter abietem atque fa- " gum (6)." Dr. Plott, however, cavils at this, vouching it as an instance of the great negligence and supine-

(1) See also what is said below on the British dogs.
(2) See my dissertation on the Coritani.
(3) See Lel. Itin. VI. p. 104, 137. The forests were numerous after the Norman conq. See Spelm. Gl. voc. FORESTA; and yet he has not mentioned all.
(4) Pliny, N. H. XVI. c. 44. " Nihil habent Druidæ... visco et arbore, " in qua gignatur (si modo sit Robur) sacratius. Jam per se Roborum eli- " gunt lucos, nec ulla sacra sine ea fronde conficiunt, &c."
(5) Wise, p. 95.
(6) Cæs. de B. G. V. c. 12.

ness with which Cæsar has conducted himself in his account of Britain, and observing the great plenty of this timber in the Chiltern (1), which also grows most freely and naturally in Kent, where the names of many places are plainly borrowed from it (2); a clear evidence of the trees flourishing there in the Saxon times. But all this notwithstanding, the beech may have been adventitious, and been brought hither from the continent since Cæsar's time. Nobody that observed how kindly this timber tree grows in the Rae wood, at Castle-Howard, would ever imagine there was not one of the sort there in Queen Elizabeth's time; and yet, I have been credibly informed, there was not.

No animal appears so frequently on our coins as the horse, and the country was deservedly famous for its horses: " I conceive, says Mr. Walker, the horse was so
" frequently stamped on their coins, because of their ex-
" traordinary goodness in this country (the like is upon
" divers cities and provinces in Gallia) or to shew that
" they were, in their own opinion, excellent horse-
" men (3)." Sometimes we have only a horse, sometimes a wheel with the horse; in which case we have reason to think the master pointed to the essedum of the Britons. Mr. Walker, however, seems to be of a different opinion;
" The wheel under him [the horse], amongst the Ro-
" mans, intimated the making of an highway for carts:
" So many of which being in the Roman times made in

(1) Plott, Oxfordsh. p. 51. and 312.
(2) As Bocton, Buckland, &c.
(3) See also Dio apud Xiphilinum, and Dr. Musgrave, I. p. 168. where he thinks horses were probably one of the British exports.

" this

COINS OF CUNOBELIN.

this country, well deserved such a memorial (1)." Dr. Plott, and Mr. Thoresby, seem to concur with him in this (2).

But as the roads were made long after this reign (3), these coins may with more reason be thought to allude to the essedum, especially as the wheel is seen upon coins that are undoubtedly Cunobelin's (4). It has been thought, the appearance of the horse indicated these coins to have been of Phœnician extraction (5); but Mr. Borlase very justly rejects that notion; and that matter is here also sufficiently cleared, since the animal occurs on the specie of this Prince, who had no dealings either with the Tyrians or Carthaginians.

It appears from Cæsar and Pomp. Mela, that the Britons in their military made use of horse, properly so called, as well as esseda; and accordingly we here see horses mounted with riders. And the horse on one coin, though not one of Cunobelin's (6), Mr. Walker thought " was fastened by one fore and the opposite hinder foot, " to some weight; as if it signified the invention of one " of their Princes, to teach them some pace or motion." One knows not what to think of a refinement so extraordinary; but nevertheless, that the Britons were very expert with their cavalry is clear, for they annoyed Cæsar very greatly with it. It is always thought allowable to argue from the manners and customs of the Gauls, to

(1) Walker, in Camd. col. CX, CXVI.
(2) Plott, Oxfordsh. p. 310. Thoresby, Mus. p. 338.
(3) See Camd. col. LXXIX. Lel. Itin. VI. p. 121.
(4) See Mr. Borlase, p. 260, 262.
(5) Idem, p. 247.
(6) Camd. I. 6.

those of the Britons; and it is believed that anciently the Gauls rode without bridles (1); from whence it is probable the Britons did so too. But in Cæsar's time, who made much use of the Gaulish cavalry, bridles were used; and Strabo mentions ivory bridles as an article imported into Britain from Gaul (2); and accordingly the horses on the coins, such as are mounted with riders, are all bridled.

To return to the wheel: Mr. Wise thinks this may denote a triumphal chariot (3); if so, it has a manifest allusion to the Roman custom, the triumph being a cavalcade entirely unknown then in this country. In one case you have the horse joined with a crescent; and quære, whether as the British Apollo was the sun, the horse was not in this instance his representative? For it must be remembered, that much of the British, or Druidical religion, was brought from the East, where the horse was sacred to the sun, according to that of Ovid,

> Placat equo Perses radiis Hyperiona cinctum,
> Ne detur celeri victima tarda Deo.
> Fast. I. 385.

In that famous representation of the destruction of the children of Niobe, by Apollo and Diana, in the Villa Medicea at Rome, a horse leaps on one of the daughters,

(1) Dodwell, de Parma Equestr. Woodw. Hearne, in Lel. Iůn. L p. 128.
(2) Strabo IV. p. 200.
(3) Wise, p. 227.

as being the favourite beaſt, and the coadjutor of Apollo in that murderous buſineſs (1).

The horſe therefore on this coin may repreſent the ſun, as the creſcent does the moon, with whom, as has been before noted, the Druids had great concern. And it is thought by etymologiſts, that the name Cunobelin is formed from Belinus, the name of a Britiſh deity correſponding with Apollo (2). Camden writes, he had ſomewhere obſerved of the god Belinus, that the Gauls worſhipped Apollo under that name. " This is confirmed, he goes on, " by Dioſcorides, who expreſly ſays, that
" the Herba Apollinaris (in the juice whereof the Gauls
" uſed to dip their arrows) was called in Gauliſh, Beli-
" nuntia. From whichI durſt almoſt make this inference,
" that the name of Cunobeline, as alſo that of Caſſibilin,
" came originally from the worſhip of Apollo, as well as
" Phœbitius and Delphidius; unleſs you ſhould rather
" ſay, that as Apollo, for his yellow hair, was called by
" the Greeks, Ξανθὸς, and by the Latins, *Flavus*; ſo he
" was called by the Britons and Gauls, *Belin:* Since a
" man of a yellow complexion, is in Britiſh called *Me-*
" *lin, Belin, Felin*; and for that reaſon, the antient
" names of Belin, Cunobelin, and Caſſibelin (called alſo
" Caſſivellaun) ſeem to import as much as *yellow*

(1) Montf. tom. I. p. 66. whom ſee II. p. 256. as likewiſe the annotators in Burman's edit. of Ovid, l. c. and Patrick on 2 Kings XXIII. 11.
(2) Montf. II. p. 263, 267. Sammes, p. 130. Alford, p. 4. Toland, p. 67, 77. Baxter, Gl. voc. BEL. Selden de Diis Syris, Synt. II. c. 1. et Beyeri Additamenta, p. 278. Mr. Hearne notes, that Apollo was in the higheſt requeſt with the Britons, Lel. Itin. VIII. p. xviii.

" *Princes*

"*Princes* (1)." The former part of the name Cun or Cuno, is thought by several to be a name of dignity (2).

Quære then, whether those circles on Cunobelin's coins, which authors so frequently call wheels, are in fact such, and are not rather representations or figures of the sun. Thus class II. no. 2. the sun is under the horse's belly, and a comet over his back, by way of explaining the meaning of the horse there. In no. 4. of that class, the crescent appears plainly in Mr. Battely's type. The crescent appears again, tho' imperfectly, class III. no. 4. and 8. and in class II. no. ult. you have the horse, with the sun, and a star of six points; and if I may be allowed, on this occasion, to cite a few coins of other Princes or states, I would refer your Lordship to Camden I. 12. where there is a star of five points; I. 25. and 26. on both which is the sun with a horse; II. 9. where there is seen sun, moon, and stars; II. 21, 31, 32. and Lord Pembroke, Part II. pl. 94. no. 9. and Battely, tab. VI. where the star of five points, with the horse and sun, occurs. Mr. Borlase, indeed, seems to doubt whether a figure on one of the Karn-Brê coins, be a crescent, saying, "It might possibly be intended to represent the golden "hook, with which their priests with so much solemnity "cut their divine misletoe, or to record the hooks or "scythes fastened to the axis of their chariots of war, for "such they had; and on these coins [of Karn-Brê] we "find several allusions to this manner of fighting (3)."

(1) Camd. col. CX. See also Alford, p. 4. and Selden, de Diis Syris, l. c. and the additamenta.
(2) See above.
(3) Borlase, p. 261.

But

COINS OF CUNOBELIN. 95

But with submission, upon our coins, they are evidently crescents. And what is most remarkable in the case, the horses on the coins here referred to are all without riders, differing in this respect from the other coins of Cunobelin; and thereby insinuating, they were not war horses, but were intended to represent something else, probably to be emblems of the sun.

The Aborigines of Britain lived much, as Cæsar tells us, upon flesh and milk: *Pecoris magnus numerus*, and again, *Interiores plerique frumenta non ferunt, sed lacte et carne vivunt, pellibusque sunt vestiti* (1). And see here on our coins the sheep and cow. Walker pretends the bull was an emblem of strength; but something more characteristical, I apprehend, is rather propounded to us by this animal; either the white bull, in so much request with the Druids, Plin. lib. XVI. c. 44, or rather their reliance on this creature for so large a part of their subsistence, and their regard and veneration for him and the cow upon that account. It appears likewise from Strabo, that Britain abounded with milk, tho' the natives had not the art of making cheese (2): And yet Mr. Hearne pretends our ancient Britons lived much upon milk and *cheese* (3). However, it is to be observed, that they had the figures of beasts or cattle cut upon their bodies (4). Your Lordship will please to observe, that Cæsar above

---

(1) See also Dio Nicæus in Xiphilinus, and Pomp. Mela III. c. 6. This was partly the case of the Suevi, Cæf. IV. 1. and the Belgæ of Gaul, Strabo IV. p. 197. and indeed of many other uncivilized nations, both antiently, and at this day.

(2) Strabo IV. p. 200.

(3) Hearne, in Lel. Itin. I. p. 124.

(4) Ibid.

speaks

speaks of the interior of Britain; for in the parts where he was chiefly conversant, there was corn (1). And I incline to think, that though in his time the Mediterranean countries had little or no experience in agriculture, yet in the reign of Cunobelin they began to practise it, imititing therein, both the Romans, and the maritime states of their own country. This may fairly be collected from the ears of corn so common upon the coins (2). Strabo says, that *some* of the Britons knew neither gardening, nor any other part of husbandry, which might be true of the most distant and least civilized parts, tho' not of the rest, since both he himself and Diod. Siculus testify, that other parts had corn; and it appears from Pliny, that in his time they manured their ground with marle (3). Viewing the spicæ upon the coins, one is very apt to fancy they represent not ears of wheat, but of barley, being so much and so apparently bearded, and the drink of the Britons being certainly made of that, as now it is with us. I shall here give your Lordship, Mr. Camden's words on this subject: " Their drink was made of barley (and so
" it is with us at this day) as Dioscorides says, who mis-
" names it Curmi for Kwrw; for so the Welsh term
" what we call Ale (4); and again, " This is our barley
" wine, which Julian the apostate ingeniously calls, in
" an epigram of his, Πυρογενῆ, ἢ ϐρόμον ὖ ϐρόμιον, *The*
" *offspring of corn, and wine without wine.* This is the
" antient and peculiar liquor of the English and Britains,

(1) Cæf. IV. 30. seq. Strabo IV. p. 199.
(2) See Camden, col. CXII.
(3) Plin. N. H. XVII. c. 6.
(4) Camd. col. XLII.

" and

COINS OF CUNOBELIN. 97

" and very wholesome it is ... one of the most learned
" men in France [Turnebus] does not question, but they
" who drink this liquor, if they avoid excess, will live
" longer than if they drank wine; and that this is the
" cause why some among us that drink ale, live to the
" age of an hundred years: Yet Asclepiades in Plutarch
" (speaking of some Britains who lived to the age of one
" hundred and twenty years) ascribes it to the coldness of
" the climate, which preserves the natural heat of their
" bodies (1)." Cunobelin, it has been observed, lived to
a great age, but the number of his years is not known.
The longævity of the Britons is ascribed by Mr. Hearne,
with much probability, to their temperance and milk
diet (2).

I shall mention but one animal more, and that is the
dog. Dr. Caius has left us a treatise de Canibus Britannicis, and it has been several times printed. Strabo notes
that the British dogs were excellent for hunting, and were
exported from hence for that purpose (3); but the species
here in question, seems to be that large and furious
animal, which the same author informs us was also an article of merchandize, as being purchased by the Celtæ or
Gauls, and entertained by them for the service of war (4).
One of those dogs was represented on a coin of Mr.
Thoresby's (5), and another is here delineated, class IV.
no. ult. as carrying a lady on his back, a proof of the

(1) Camden, col. 588.
(2) Lel. Itin. I. p. 124.
(3) Strabo IV. p. 199.
(4) Strabo IV. p. 200.
(5) Described in his Mus. p. 338.

O strength

strength and size of this mastiff. The learned Camden, my Lord, has a notable passage concerning the British dogs; but, as it is too long to transcribe, I shall content myself with referring your Lordship to him (1). However, I may remark, that in Montfaucon, tom. II. plate 58. you have the representation of " a combat between a " lion and some other animal ; which, by reason of the " poorness of the graving, is scarce distinguishable, toge- " ther with an inscription, BELLICVS SVRBVR, altogether " as barbarous as the figures." This is the account the author there gives of it. The word BELLICVS is written under what he calls the lion, but in my opinion is one of the British dogs of the mastiff and fighting kind, carried to Gaul, or one of that breed; the name *Bellicus* being well adapted to a beast of such strength and courage, as we must suppose those were which the Gauls employed in their wars. The other animal, which the dog is going to encounter, if we may judge from the type, is undoubtedly a boar; the word written underneath it, SVRBVR, seems to imply as much, from BERRES, *i. e.* VERRES (2), or *Bora*, the Cornish word for a boar (3), and SVR denoting great; or, if you will admit SVR to be for SVS, the s changed into R, as in E. Lhuyd, p. 30. and Baxt. Gl. voc. ADMINIVS, BORR may then signify *magnus*, as in Lhuyd, p. 84. SVRBVR in both cases will mean *a great boar*.

I turn now to something else. These coins are alloyed with lead and tin, the latter of which, did we want his au-

(1) Camd. col. 139. See also Lewis, p. 55. seq.
(2) Idem Tit. VIII. p. 271. voc. BOAR.
(3) E. Lhuyd, Tit. II. voc. APER. Borlase's Corn. Engl. Vocab. voc. BORA.

thority,

COINS OF CUNOBELIN.

thority, Cæsar says, grew in the island (1); but the Cassiterides including, in the opinion of most, the county of Cornwall, as well as the Scilly islands, is an everlasting proof of this. The lead of Britain is particularly mentioned in Pliny (2). One of the British coins, but not known to be Cunobelin's, is of iron (3), a metal found here in Cæsar's time (4).

Cæsar tells us, the Britons wore their hair long, but shaved it in every part of the body, except the head and the upper lip, " Capilloque sunt promisso; atque omni " parte corporis rasa, præter caput et labrum superius:" And yet there are no signs of this flowing hair upon the coins, the reason of which, I apprehend, may be, that the Princes were exempt from this general rule. Another instance, parallel to this, may not be improperly mentioned in this place. The same author says, the inland Britons were *habited with skins, pellibusque sunt vestiti*; a representation which, I think, ought to be restrained to the common sort of people, the Princes and the Druids (5) being better clad, as is evident from the appearance Cunobelin makes on the coins. The vulgar indeed had a substantial reason for shewing as much of their bodies as they could; which was, that they died their skins with woad, either for the sake of looking more terrible in bat-

(1) Nascitur ibi plumbum album in Mediterraneis regionibus, in maritimis ferrum. Cæs. V. 12.
(2) Lib. XXXIV. c. 17.
(3) Thoresby, p. 337.
(4) Cæs. l. c.
(5) Pliny, N. H. XVI. c. 44. Sacerdos candida veste cultus arborem scandit. See him again, XXIV. c. 11. and Montf. tom. II. p. 278. sect. 3. Jones's answers to Mr. Tate's questions in Hearne's Cur. Disc. p. 216.

tle (1), or for ornament and beauty (2). Hence Herodian exprefly fays, ὅθεν ἐ δ' ἀμφιέννυνται, ἵνα μὴ σκέπωσι τῦ σώμα[τ]Θ- τὰς γραφάς. *For this reafon they go uncloath'd; namely, that they may not hide the figures made on their bodies* (3). Whence it appears, that the fkins ufed by the common people, covered them not fo much before as behind: And if it would not be thought a repetition, I would alfo note, that the cafe was fimilar in refpect of defenfive armour; that the common or private men only engaged unarmed (4), whilft the Princes, or other officers, had their fhields and helmets, as Cunobelin has on the coins. But to return from this digreffion; the Britons wore no beards, and the coins accordingly are without them, which perhaps might be one reafon why the heads of Janus and Hercules, as above, appear with none. 'Tis a particular worth remarking, becaufe, as it feems to me, it was the abfence of the beard that induced Walker, in certain cafes, to call the heads, women's heads. I make no doubt but the Britons in common wore their hair long; " The Gauls were called *Comati*, " from their long hair. The Britons had probably the " fame cuftom [it may be affirmed they had] for all un- " cultivated nations wore long hair, except the *Alani*, " (Lucian I ox). It was an inftance of their wildnefs," fays Mr. Borlafe (5). The cafe was the fame with the Belgæ of Gaul (6).

(1) Atque hoc horridiore funt in pugna adfpectu. Cæf. V. 14.
(2) See Oudendorp ad Cæf. l. c.
(3) Herodian III. c. 47.
(4) See above, p. 65.
(5) Borlafe, p. 263.
(6) Strabo IV. p. 196. et Cafaub. ad loc.

A3

COINS OF CUNOBELIN.

As for the diadem, we make no difficulty in afcribing the laureate one to the Roman or Romanized artift. The other kinds may feem neceffary, where the hair was to be dreffed, and not fuffered to grow difhevell'd. In fome of the Karn-Brê coins, the diadem is plain and ftrong, as on fome of ours; but, neverthelefs, there is one remarkable difference between our diadems, and thofe on the Greek and Roman coins; " for, whereas, in the laft
" mentioned ('tis the obfervation of Mr. Borlafe) the fillet
" or ribband on which the diadem is grounded (or by
" which 'tis bound together) makes a very elegant knot
" behind the head, the Britifh coins have no fuch
" thing, but have a ftraight bandage, or rather clafp,
" which croffes the diadem at right angles; and was
" doubtlefs defigned (like the fillet of the antients) to
" keep the diadem firm in its place, and clofe to the
" head (1)." This clafp, indeed, does not appear on our coins, but the former part of the obfervation accords therewith. Mr Selden moreover remarks, that the diadem which he produces feems to be of pearl.

Our Britons were remarkable for their dexterity in the ufe of the fpear or javelin (2), and particularly from their horfes and chariots; and here we fee the horfeman with his fpear.

As for the Britifh fhields, they feem to have been lozenges, clafs V. no. 4. Mr. Camden does not defcribe that which he faw; fee him col. CXII. and the Gallic fhields in Montfaucon II. p. 270. are hexagons; but Mr.

(1) Id. ibid.
(2) Cæf. IV. 24. feq. Dio apud Xiphilinum.

Hearne

Hearne tells us, the thyreos of the Gauls was an oblong, and the cetrum a short sort of shield (1).

It may be proper to mention here, that the Druids were eminent for their skill in botany. Pliny relates some of their superstitious practices in relation to the *Viscus*, or misletoe of the oak, the *Selego*, and *Samolus*; and Dioscorides tells us, that the Gauls, meaning, no doubt, the Gaulish Druids, called the Herba Apollinaris, *Belinuntia*. Cæsar, and several other authors, mention the vitrum or woad, wherewith the Britons dyed their bodies; and possibly the flower on class V. no. 2, 3. may be intended to represent to us, either the flower of this plant, or of some one of the above; but I am not botanist enough to determine which. Walker however, my Lord, will inform you, that it is no uncommon thing to see the names or figures of plants upon antient coins. See the commentary on no. 2. class VI.

As for the British pearls, concerning which the antients, and even the more modern authors, have said so much, the pearl diadem is mentioned above, and Mr. Borlase found them on the manes of the horses (2); but they are not very conspicuous on our coins in that place. I take them to have been the growth of the more Northern part of the island.

But I should weary your Lordship, were I to proceed any further in this induction of particulars; and therefore, to wind up my bottom, I shall only add, that the true original orthography of the name of Cunobelin's pa-

---

(1) Hearne, in Lel. Itin. I. p. 124.
(2) See him passim.

lace, was Camulodunum, which ought to be particularly mentioned; becaufe Mr. Camden, tho' he was aware of the authority of the coins, and even produces them on the occafion, yet feems to prefer Camalodunum, ufing this orthography as an argument for fixing Camulodunum at Malden (1). Authors, it feems, give it both ways; wherefore, as Camulodunum has its friends, as this correfponds fo well with the etymology, and is fupported alfo by the evidence of no lefs than three coins, we have reafon to prefer it, as I think moft do (2).

On the fame footing, I fhould imagine, the Celtic name of Apollo was Bilinus, or rather Belinus, and not Belenus, notwithftanding the name is given in the laft form in authors (3), not Bellinus, as fometimes we fee it written; this arifing, as we think, from pronunciation, the e being fhort (4). Some have thought the numerals of this name, might exprefs the number of days in the year, as Abraxas and Meithras do (5); but there is no foundation for this, if either Belinus or Bilinus be the orthography; and indeed it is no artificial word, but has an etymology (6).

So again, what later authors write *Venta*, as Venta Silurum, &c. was at this time written *Vamita*. The Trinobantes of Cæfar appear to have been alfo called Novantes; and if Cearatic be not the name of another of Cunobelin's foreign mint-mafters, as may be fufpected, it is the

(1) Camden, col. 416.
(2) Gibfon, in Camd. col. 417. Alford, p. 6.—Baxter, p. 64. blames Mr. Camden for preferring Camalodunum.
(3) Montfaucon II. p. 267.
(4) Montfaucon, ibid.
(5) Montfaucon, ibid.
(6) Selden, de Diis Syris.

name of one of his towns, ranking with Verulam and Camulodunum, as *mcv* is another.

But I shall trouble your Lordship no further, than to say I have the honour of being

Your Lordship's,

Whitington,
March 30, 1765.

most obliged,

and most devoted Servant,

SAMUEL PEGGE.

P. S. Our antiquaries, I find, are very generally of opinion, my Lord, that the English words *Task* and *Tax*, come from this old British *Tascia*, interpreted by them tribute money. Thus Mr. Baxter writes, " De Britan-
" norum veterum *Tascia* nata sunt Anglorum vocabula
" *Task* et *Tax*." Baxter, Gloss. voc. TASCIA, and in Mr. Wise, p. 226. and thus Dr. Pettingal above, " The meer
" English word *Tax*, is perhaps a corruption of *Task*.—
" Task is derived from *Tascia* of the antient Britons; and
" Tascia was the vectigal or tribute paid by the *Tag*, or
" British Prince of each province, to the Roman con-
" querors (1)." But certainly there is no occasion to go so far for the original of these words, since *Task* comes so easily from the French *Tasche*, it being agreeable to the idiom of the English tongue to harden the French *ch*: Thus we have *clock* from *cloche*, *pocket* from *pochette*, &c. As to the word *Tax*, Dr. Pettingal has clearly shewn

(1) See also Alford, p. 4.

It

it cannot come from the claſſical ſenſe of *Taxatio*; but, neverthelefs, it may take its origin from *Taxare*, of the baſe latinity; a word, which with the noun *Taxa*, occurs perpetually in our Monkiſh writers. It can hardly be conceived, my Lord, what a number of words have been adopted into our language, from the barbariſms of the Monks. But theſe are not of this place; and I only mention it to ſhew the probability of the etymon here propoſed, and that *Taxa, Taxare*, and *Taxatio*, are not, as might otherwiſe be ſurmiſed, the Engliſh word *Tax* latinized.

The French *Taſcher*, to endeavour, from whence I preſume their *Taſche* may come, may be, for ought we know, of Celtic original; and if *Taſcio* can be thought to bear any relation to it, it will then ſignify a trial or eſſay, a ſenſe very conſiſtent with what has been above advanced, viz. That theſe coins of Cunobelin were the firſt productions of the Britiſh mints; and, in my opinion, my Lord, a much more reaſonable ſuppoſition and interpretation, and a more ſenſible one, than that *Taſcio* ſhould mean tribute-money. The reader is at liberty, if he pleaſes, to take this ſenſe of the word; but, for my own particular, I muſt needs ſay, it is more agreeable to my notions of things, that *Taſcio* ſhould be the name of the mint-maſter, this being ſo conformable, as I think has been remarked, to the practice of the Franks and Saxons afterwards, and alſo accounting ſo well for the Greekiſh and Romanizing types ſo apparent on our coins.

P   I have

I have learned, my Lord, since the penning of this Essay, that the late Dr. Stukeley has left a work behind him upon the same subject. The Doctor, I am sensible, has his admirers; but I must confess I am not one of the number, as not being fond of wildness and enthusiasm upon any subject. The present attempt, however, needs not to preclude the Doctor's piece, no more than his, which is probably on a different plan (for I don't often think alike with Dr. Stukely) ought to supersede it. On the contrary, I shall read what he has been pleased to offer on this subject with avidity, and, as I hope, with candour.

ADDENDA.

ADDENDA.

Page 34. *l. ult. after* mentioned, *add :* in the several various readings.

Page 54. *l. antepenult. after the words* from our Island. *add :* Nay we have Q. DOCI on a silver Celtic coin in Lord Pembroke, Part II. Tab. 93. where the prænomen plainly indicates a Roman master; wherefore methinks when the Celtic coins in that table present us with DONNVS, LIMA, &c. these probably may be the names of masters also, not strictly Roman, but provincial; just as I suppose the case to have been with Tascio. On two of these coins struck at Tournay, and exhibiting the head of that town, after the Roman manner, the master's name occurs in the same form with ours, viz. AVSCRO.

Page 63. *l.* 7. Caratacus. *add* see above, p. 57.

Page 66. *l. ult. add :* My learned friend, Mr. John Watson of Ripponden, near Halifax, in Yorkshire, has a gold coin, of much the same type with this, and was so obliging as to send me a drawing of it; but as the variations (which consist in ◎ being under the horse's belly over CVN, and not before the horse's head as in Camden) are not material, it was not worth while to engrave it.

Page 67. *l.* 16. something. *add :* It seems to be a garland or Civic crown.

Page 78. *l. antepen.* The coins delineated and described, are now above forty; for the observation there made,

made, that the number of the coins of Cunobelin would probably in procefs of time be much greater, when new coins were difcovered, and thofe now latent in the cabinets of the curious were more generally brought to light, has been in part very happily verified by the humanity and friendfhip of Mr. John White, the fame gentleman to whom I formerly addreffed the *third* letter in the *Series of Differtations on our Anglo-Saxon Remains*. Mr. White no fooner heard of the prefent defign, but, from the benevolence of his difpofition, and a moft laudable communicablenefs, he inftantly wrote to apprize me of fuch coins of Cunobelin as were in his collection (a collection as extenfive as elegant, and altogether moft princely and magnificent); and in the moft obliging and generous manner to offer me drawings of thofe that, hitherto being unengraved or undefcribed, might prove accommodate to my purpofe.

Thefe coins of Mr. White, in number four, have therefore been fince added to the plates, where, as it fortuned, they fell into their refpective places without offending the eye; and your Lordfhip will find them marked with the letters a. b. c. d. But as the fheets of the Effay had paffed the prefs before they came to hand, particularly thofe that contain the commentary or defcription of the coins, p. 64. feq. it will be neceffary I fhould go over them in this place, but with the fame brevity as was ufed in refpect of the others.

Clafs I. a. is a gold coin with a blank reverfe. The obverfe has a good horfe upon the gallop; over him a hand dexter holding a truncheon with a pearl, or pellet, at a fmall diftance from each end of it; and underneath him

him a wrigling ferpent. The infcription CVNO. Some perhaps may query, upon a view of the type of this coin, whether the horfe was not once mounted, and the hand did not belong to a rider, imagining the piece may be worn in that part. All I can fay, is, that though the hand and truncheon is entirely very fingular, yet there is no appearance of any other other part of a horfeman, or larger figure, in the draught, and that I take the horfe, therefore, to be emblematical in this cafe, as obferved, p. 92. feq. and to reprefent Apollo, or the fun. The ferpent is a frequent attribute of Apollo, as the God of medicine, under which character he was known to the Britons, fee above, p. 44. But whether he was fo or not, Tafcio was well aware of his medical power, and might, therefore, adorn him very properly with his enfign. Britain at this time was not without its ferpents, as may be inferred from the adder-beads, or fnake ftones, of the Druids (1), and what fome old authors remark concerning certain parts of it, as particularly the Ifle of Thanet, being deftitute of them, as an extraordinary and exclufive privilege (2). The truncheon, however, as an emblem of command, may probably be thought to come from Rome, and, therefore, to be a pure device of Tafcio's; it affords us confequently a further example of the Roman manners and implements introduced here by him. As for the pearls, or pellets, in the area of this coin, fee above, p. 102.

(1) Camden's Brit. col. 815. feq.
(2) Solinus, Beda, &c.

Clafs

Class II. b. The obverse of this gold coin, with CVNOB, seems plainly to me to give us the bust of Jupiter Ammon, for the horn is very evident, as also is the venerable beard of that deity. These are particulars that absolutely restrain us from complimenting Cunobelin with this well-wrought head, since the horn is characteristic, and the Britons always went shaved, see above, p. 99. Indeed it was there advanced, that the British princes might be exempt from general rules in point of dress; but we have good reason for believing they were not particular as to the beard, since Cunobelin is universally beardless upon the coins. Now if Tascio, my Lord, was a provincial of Gaul, as conjectured above (1), he could be no stranger to the deities of Ægypt and Africa, whatever the Britons might be, for they abounded in Gaul. He, therefore, was probably the first person that imported the knowledge of this Libyan divinity into Britain. And whereas the reverse of this elegant coin has a lion couchant (for such I esteem it to be) an animal unknown in this island, the same hand may reasonably be supposed to depict it as a native of Libya, and connected with Jupiter Ammon, though an artist of Britain could not possibly have any idea of it. CAM, the letters on this reverse, we interpret Camulodunum; and this seems but reasonable, though the name of the place is generally given more at large, CAMV, or CAMVL.

Class IV. c. This brass coin, which is in the finest and most perfect preservation, has the king mounted; the

(1) Page 54.

horse

horse upon the gallop, and bridled (1). 'Tis difficult to say what the prince holds in his right hand, whether a whip, or something wherewith to annoy the enemy; but as he is unarmed I should imagine the former, see Class V. N° 2. and p. 38. The inscription is CVNO. The reverse has the prince again on foot, with a helmet, spear, and shield. I esteem it to be the figure of the prince, and not a soldier, because of the helmet, &c. for the common people of Britain did not, as I apprehend, at this time make use of defensive armour (2). The inscription on the reverse TASC NO is probably the same as *Tasc nova*, and *Tasc novane*, that is, *Tasc novanetum*, concerning which, see before, p. 72. seq.

Class V. d. This silver coin presents us, on the obverse, with another creature of the imagination, to wit, a griffin running, of which the Britons probably had no notion at this time, but must be indebted for it to our foreign artist. This creature, as I remember, was sacred to the god Mars (3), or Camulus, the favourite and patron of Cunobelin, and consequently appears with the utmost propriety upon his money. The reverse has a Pegasus, for which see p. 46; and the inscription here, there being none on the obverse, is TAS for Tascio. The coin is extremely perfect, as indeed all in Mr. White's collection in general are.

(1) See page 92.
(2) See page 65. 100.
(3) Gentleman's Magazine.

ADDENDA.

Page 89. *l.* 7. *after* others. *add:* It is very opportunely remarked by Mr. Morant, in the Antiquities of Colchester, p. 11. seq. that even the country about Camulodunum, the place of Cunobelin's more immediate residence, and where many of the coins were struck, was in his time very generally covered with wood.

Page 102. *l.* 2. a short sort of shield. *add:* The truth seems to be, that the British shields were of various forms, since that of Class VI. N° 2. is an oval.

ERRATA.

Page 10. line 19. *after* all *add* the
Ib. Note *for* word *r.* world
11. 19. does not *r.* dares not
13. 18. and 20. Note (1) belongs to (2) and *vice versâ.*
22. 13. prince, chief, *r.* prince or chief,
23. 4. deviation *r.* derivation
28. 19. J *should be only a comma.*
33. 4. Tarraconienses, *r.* Conenienses,
44. Note (1) 20. *r.* 22.
Note (3) *dele* Hearne is
45. 5. The Graeian Hercules, *a new paragraph.*
54. 28. it is, *r.* as it is,
58. 13. Caractarus, *r.* Caratacus,
63. *penult.* and several particulars more fully examined, *r.* and fully examined several other particulars,
67. 22. CVNO, *r.* CVN,
72. *penult.* CVNOBRLIN, *r.* CVNOBILIN,
81. 18. Cassivellauni, *r.* the Cassivellauni,
82. 1. servied; *semicolon should be only a comma,*
98. Note (a) Idem *r.* E. Lhuyd,
102. 6. Salopa, *r.* Salopa,
103. 14. not *r.* nor

A DIS-

A
DISSERTATION
ON
THE CORITANI.

Of the Etymology and Orthography of that Name, and the Extent and true Situation of this People;

Of the Caledonian Wood in the Midland Parts of Britain;

Paffages of L. Florus and Pliny concerning it, and the Etymology of that Word;

Likewife of the Caledonian Bears;

Of the Limits in refpect of the Brigantes and Carnabii; and herein of the Name and Extraction of the Iceni, of whom the Coritani were a Part;

And fhewing, againft Dr. Plot, that they were not feated in Worcefterfhire and Staffordfhire.

[Read to the Society of Antiquaries, April 5 and 12, 1764.]

Q

TO

MATTHEW DUANE, Esquire.

SIR,

AS some notice has been taken in the foregoing essay, page 89. of the immense wilds and forests of Britain, and the three vast Caledonian woods were there particularly mentioned, with a reference to a dissertation of mine on the seat of the Coritani, which was partly made public by its having been read at the Society of Antiquaries, but nevertheless is not generally known, it was thought proper to annex that dissertation for the reader's further amusement. And as you, Sir, was pleased to express your approbation of it at the time it was read, I beg leave to present you with it in this public manner, as a testimony of that regard wherewith I am, SIR,

  Your most obedient,

   and obliged Servant,

      SAMUEL PEGGE.

December 26, 1763.

WHEN the Romans arrived in Britain they found a people settled in the inland parts, whom they distinguished by the name of *Coritani* (1); a word formed, no doubt, from the British appellation of this people, whatever that was. This name appears in Ptolemy, who stiles them Κοριτανοὶ, *i. e.* Coritani, as the Latin version of that author, and Mr. Camden in his Britannia, give it very justly; for whereas Ptolemy mentions the cities Λίνδον and Ῥάγε, Lincoln and Leicester, as seated in this clan, these two places occur in the region of the *Coltanni* in Richard of Cirencester (2), as Lindum also again does in his map. And yet Mr. Baxter would attempt to read the word in Ptolemy otherwise: "CORRGAUNI, five malles *Coriceni*, Ptolemæo vitiose "scribuntur Κοριτάυοι pro Κοριγαύνοι, de quo ex Latino "Interprete Camdenus fecit *Coritani*." But it appears evidently enough, that both the interpreter and Camden have called this people very properly from Ptolemy, Coritani, as supposing the *Ypsilon* to be miswritten for *Nu*.

As to the etymology of this term, Mr. Camden offers his conjecture with the utmost diffidence: " I " shall forbear, says he, to meddle with the etymology

---

(1) The true orthography of this name will be attempted below.
(2) Richard of Cirencester, p. 26.

" of

" of the name, left I should pretend to know what,
" in truth, is to me a mystery. For, notwithstanding
" they are a people scattered *far and wide*, which the
" Britons express by *Gur-tani*, yet, should I assert that
" these Goritani took their name from thence, would
" you not think this meer trifling? They who are bet-
" ter skilled in that way, may give their conjectures
" with greater safety (1). Mr. Baxter has accordingly
pronounced more magisterially: " Hi minores erant
" *Iceni* sive *Igauni* sive etiam *Uigantes* : nam ejusmodi
" Composita in hunc diem Britannis sunt familiaria,
" uti cernere est in *Cornant, Corgi, Corbedii,* atque
" his similibus (2)." So that to get his word *Corigauni*,
he is forced, besides the attack upon Ptolemy, as above,
to corrupt the word *Iceni* into *Igauni* or *Uigantes*, which
methinks is rather too bold and arbitrary. But, what
will become of the former part of the composition
should Richard of Cirencester's reading, *Coitanni,* prove
to be the true one? This shall be considered bye and
bye. Mr. Baxter proceeds, " In Ravennati Libro di-
" cuntur *Corii;* in Graeco certe exemplari. Ράτας Κοριων
" fuerat ; unde et Latina versio suum *Ratae Corion*
" traxit." He supposes, and yet I know not upon what
grounds, the anonymous geographer of Ravenna, to

---
(1) Camden's Britannia, col. 311.
(2) Baxter's Gloss. v. CORIGAUNI. Afterwards he says, " Neque praeter-
" eundum hoc loco censeo *Icenos* in Taciti libris mendose dici *Jugantes*, ex-
" scriptorum vitio pro *Uigantes*: ut sint *Corigani* Britannis antiquis *Corüigan,*
" sive *Coriiigantes,* hodierna prolatione *Corüycbon,* sive *Corüycbont*; nam
" et pluralia in *on* antiquitus etiam desinebant in *ont,* quod vel Latinizata
" nomina ostendunt."

have

have tranflated his work from a Greek original; but be that as it will, who fees not, that the *Ratecorion* of that author (1), is an abbreviation of *Ratæ Coritanorum*, written thus *Corion*, as Dr. Gale has remarked? If this be the cafe, as moft people will think it is, fince both Ptolemy and Richard place *Ragæ* amongft the *Coritani* or *Coitanni*, the Coritani are not called *Corii* by this geographer, nor indeed by any other author, though Mr. Baxter affects afterwards to call them by that name (2).

The authority of the geographer of Ravenna added to that of Ptolemy above, fince both of them infert *R* in the former part of this word, may feem to make it clear, that the true name of this people amongft the Romans was *Coritani* (3): and yet I have fome doubt of this, and I fhall the more readily propofe my fcruple, becaufe it will lead to to what I have to offer concerning its etymon. Richard of Cirencefter perpetually calls this people *Coitanni*, and that both in his work and in his map. But as this perfon is at prefent but little known, and I propofe hereafter to make confiderable ufe of him, it will be neceffary I fhould here fpeak fomething further concerning him and his authority.

Richard was a monk of Weftminfter, though born at Cirencefter, and flourifhed, as has been fhewn by Dr. Stukely, who gave us the firft printed account of him (4),

(1) Anon. Ravennas, p. 145. Edit. Gale.
(2) See below in that page.
(3) Our Antiquaries in general all write it fo.
(4) Printed at London, 1757. Quarto.

at the close of the fourteenth century, for he died, as is supposed, A. D. 1400 or 1401. His *Commentariolum Geographicum de situ Britaniæ et stationum quas Romani ipsi in ea insula ædificaverunt*, was published entire by Mr. Charles Bertram, at Copenhagen, A. D. 1757, octavo, from a manuscirpt that came accidentally into his hands. You observe that Richard writes professedly upon the geography of this island; and though he is but a late writer, in respect of the times we are here speaking of, yet, as he has informed us, he compiled his book from certain antient memorials, his authority consequently in that view ought to be deemed very considerable; indeed, the number of places recorded by him, and unknown to all our other authors, are a full proof that he wrote from membranes which they had not seen: but take his own words, " Ex fragmentis quibusdam a *duce quodam*
" *Romano* consignatis et posteritati relictis sequens col-
" lectum est Itinerarium, ex Ptolemæo et aliunde non-
" nullis: ordinem quoque, sed, quod spero, in melius
" mutatum hinc inde deprehendes (1)."

Richard, it seems, for I now return to the subject, wrote his Commentary with Ptolemy before him, and yet he chuses to call this people constantly and invariably, as was observed, by the name of *Caltanni*, a word very naturally deducible from the British *Coit*, a wood. This clan being in all probability so denominated from that immense forest called *Sylva Caledonia* so visible in Richard's map, and of which he writes thus, p. 26. " Ex altera parte ad
" Ausonam incolebant, Carnabiis Brigantibus et oceano

(1) Ric. Corinensis, p. 35.

" vicini,

"vicini, Coitanni, *in tractu sylvis obsito*, qui, ut aliæ Britonum Sylvæ, Caledonia fuit appellata." It adds great confirmation to the conjecture, that the city of Lincoln, mentioned above as lying in this tract, was called by the Britons *Caer-Lind-Coit* (1).

The point next to be considered, is, what extent of country, the Coitanni might anciently occupy; "Hodie," says Mr. Baxter, "Coriorum Pagus Leircestriæ dicitur conventus." But what? they extended farther than this? Yes, for he writes afterwards, that the shepherds of this clan were possessed of the present county of Derby; "Ad horum [Coriorum] *Ceangos* sive pastores, spectasse videntur et lati Antoniani Campi (2) et Derventionensis etiam conventus, qua de re plura in voce CEANGI." Mr. Camden's account is more accurate. The Coritani, he tells us, joined to the Iceni, but were more within land, "taking up a very large tract of ground in the middling part of the isle, and as far as the German ocean; viz. the counties commonly called Northamptonshire, Leicestershire, Rutlandshire, Lincolnshire, Nottinghamshire, and Derbyshire." Leicestershire was therefore only a part of the Coritani, as Derbyshire was another part. The limits of the several counties abovementioned did very exactly coincide with the boundaries of the Coritani, except that they seem to have inhabited a small portion of the southern part or west-riding of Yorkshire, as will be noted below, and not to have occupied the whole

(1) Camden, col. 562.
(2) Called so from the river Antona or Aufona in Northamptonshire.

of Northamptonshire, but only to have inhabited northward from the river Aufona or Avon. In short, the most perfect account of the site of this people must be fetched from Richard of Cirencester, who writes, that the Coitanni were not so properly joined to the Iceni, as a *part* of that powerful people, who consisted of two clans, the Cenomanni (1), or Cenimagni as Cæsar calls them, and the Coitanni. " Limes huic populo [*i. e.* " Trinobantibus*]* ad Septentrionem flumen Surius, " ultra quem habitabant Iceni celeberrima natio, in " *duas partes* divisa." The river Stour parts the county of Essex from Suffolk (2), which shews we ought in this place to read *Sturius* for *Surius* (3), and so the author writes the name of this river, p. 37. The author goes on to speak of the two clans the Iceni consisted of, " quarum prior, Cenomanni, habitans ad Septentrionem " Trinobantes et Cassios [lege, Trinobantum et Cassi- " orum] ad orientem Oceanum spectabat —— flumi- " num notissima sunt Garion, Surius (4) et Aufona in " sinum Metorin sese exonerans." Now follows the description of the Coitanni. " Ex altera parte ad " Aufonam incolebant, Carnabiis et Oceano vicini, " Coitanni, in tractu sylvis obsito, qui, ut aliæ Brit- " tonum sylvæ, Caledonia fuit appellata. De hac " autem ll. mentionem facit Historicus ille Florus. " Civitas primaria Coitannorum erat Ragæ, et præter

(1) So Richard always writes.
(2) See Mr. Hearne, ad Spelm. Life of K. Ælfred, p. 74.
(3) As also again in the passage cited below.
(4) See Note 3.

" hanc

"hanc Romanorum colonia Lindum, in extrema ad orientem Provinciæ ora. Totam vero regionem bifariam fecat fluvius Trivona."

The Coitanni, therefore, bordered on the Brigantes, who lived in the country now called Yorkshire, northward; the German ocean eastward; the Cenomanni on the south, from whom they were parted by the river Aufona; and the Carnabii, who lived in Staffordshire and Cheshire, on the west. The same is also verified by the old map added by this author, and the course of the river Trent, here called Trivona, which does in a manner, especially in this author's conception, as explained by his map (1), run through the middle of the Coitanni.

The author here mentions the *Caledonian* wood or forest, which he represents as a common appellative amongst the Britons for a wood, and as particularly taken notice of by the Roman historian Luc. Florus in his third book.

In regard to Florus, he speaks of the *Saltus Caledonius* (2) in his first book, along with the *Saltus Hercynius*, in a proverbial way, as a forest of vast extent, and as yet unpassed. Mr. Camden, indeed, places the *Saltus Caledonius* of Florus in Scotland (3), but it was more probably either the wood Anderida, which was called

---

(1) Richard's Course of the Trent is very particular; see the Map, and Dr. Stukeley's Account, p. 25.
(2) Or, *Caledonius*; for see Duker ad loc. Tacitus, Ptolemy, and Pliny.
(3) Britannia, col. 1227.

also Caledonia (1), or this immense woody tract of the *Coitanni*; however, this last I am firmly persuaded was the Sylva Caledonia intended by Pliny, when he writes that the Romans had penetrated no farther into this country in his time (2). Florus, in his third book, speaks of Julius Cæsar's following the Britons *in Calidonias Sylvas*, and taking one of their kings prisoner. Now Julius never proceeded far into Britain, as the annotators there remark (3), from whence it appears that this Sylva of the *Coitanni* was not intended in that place, though our author Richard pretends it was, but rather the wood Anderida before-mentioned; for I am more willing to believe that Florus speaks of a real wood, than to imagine with Rupertus, that the author here speaks by a poetical figure (4). Now as to Richard's remark that Calidonia was a common name amongst the Britons for a wood, we find one of this name amongst the *Coitanni*, another in the country of the Cantii and Regni, otherwise called Anderida, and a third in Scotland (5). It seems, indeed, to have been a general word amongst the Celtæ, witness, Calydna, Calydon, &c. for which see the geographers. In regard to Britain, the word grew so common among the Roman authors, as Mr. Camden observes, that they made use of it to express all Britain, *and all the forests of Britain* (6).

(1) Richard of Cirenc. p. 18.
(2) Romanis armis non ultra vicinitatem Silvæ Caledoniæ propagantibus. Plin. N. H. IV. c. 16.
(3) See also Camden, col. 1227. and col. lii.
(4) See Dukeri Annot. ad loc.
(5) Camden, col. 1227. 1247.
(6) Ibid.

THE CORITANI.

There are two etymologies given of this word, the first by Mr. Camden, where he is speaking of the Caledonii in Scotland, who, he thinks, "were so called of *Kaled*, a British word signifying *bard*, which in the plural number is *Kaledion*; whence *Caledonii*, that is, a people *hardy, rough, uncivilized, wild and rustick*, such as the northern people generally are; of a fierce temper, from the extreme coldness of their climate; and bold and forward, from their abundance of blood. And besides their climate, the nature of the country contributes to it, rising up every where in *rough* and *rugged* mountains; and mountaineers are known by all to be a *hardy* and *robust* people." But this etymon seems rather foreign to the purpose, there being nothing in it peculiar to woods and forests, though I find it much approved by Lloyd in his dictionary (1). I would, therefore, rather embrace the following derivation of Mr. Baxter, as more agreeable to the observation of Richard of Cirencester; "Dicti sunt *Caledones*, says Baxter, "de *Sylvis* quas incolebant, Britannis nostris *Kelydbon* sive *Colydbon*, atque ipsæ eorum *sylvæ*, *Coit Kelydbon*: neque sane aliunde peregrini Brigantes audiebant Κέλται, nisi quòd in *Sylvis* agerent (ut fere antiqui) sicuti neque *Caletes* Atrebatum *Sylvis* vicinus populus. Scotobrigantibus etiam hodie *Coil* pro *Sylva* est; Græcis etiam Κᾶλον *Lignum* est,

(1) Dict. Hist. Geogr. in voce.

"ut

" ut et Romanis antiquis *Cala*, unde et *Caliga* et *Calo-*
" *nes* deducta funt (1)."

The enormous extent of this wood has been already often noticed; it seems by Richard's map to have covered the whole country of the *Coitanni*, and consequently to have included the whole of the prefent county of Derby, which greatly fupports Mr. Baxter's etymon; and when Dr. Stukely explains it of Rockingham foreft in Northamptonfhire, it is not greatly amifs, that being a part, though but a fmall part, of it. From hence very probably came thofe Britifh bears of which we read fo much in authors (2), and called exprefly by Martial *Urfi Caledonii* (3). The author of the panegyric to Conftantine pretends the woods of *Britain have no favage beafts* (4); but this muft be a meer flower of rhetoric, fince the evidence is fo ftrong againft him. Some indeed have fancied that the word *urfus* fignified any furious wild beaft (5); but this has been fhewn to be a miftake by the excellent Salmafius (6), and in truth, when one reflects on the other fpecies of animals that have been either loft or deftroyed in this ifland, concerning which

(1) Baxter's Gloff. v. CALEDONIA; and as to the Irifh word *Coil*, fee Ed. Lhuyd's Compar. Vocab. p. 143. 160.
(2) Plutarch. Nennius c. 62. Geoffr. Monm. p. 319. Camden, col. 462. 771. 1020. 1227. Ray on the Deluge, p. 174. compared with p. 208. whence it appears that *Bevers* there fhould be *Bears*. The Britifh name Arthur, comes from *Arth*, urfus; *Arth urryu* being a He Bear: fee Lhuyd's Comp. Vocab. v. *Urfus*.
(3) Martial de Spectac. Epigr. VII.
    " Nuda Caledonio fic pectora præbuit urfo."
(4) Camden, col. iv.
(5) Juft. Lipfius Elect. Lib. II. c. 4.
(6) Salmafii Plin. Exerc. p. 221.

see Mr. Lhuyd in Camden, col. 771. one has no reafon to difbelieve the exiftence of thefe animals here formerly. The queftion then is, whether the Caledonian bears came from the *Coitannian* wood, or the Caledonian wood in Scotland. Mr. Camden (1) and Dr. Stukeley (2) fetch the Caledonian bear mentioned by Martial from Caledonia in Scotland, and the latter of thefe authors in particular brings his epigram in proof of the Romans having conquered Scotland by the conduct of their great general Julius Agricola; but the argument is far from being conclufive, fince the bear there mentioned might with equal probability be bred amongft the *Coitanni*, and be ftiled Caledonian from the Sylva Caledonia in that part of Britain. But of this let gentlemen judge.

The ifland of Britain being in thefe antient times inhabited by various ftates independent one of another (3), thefe ftates would frequently unite in oppofing a common enemy, but not always with that unanimity as was neceffary (4), and their divifions, as has been frequently obferved, in the event proved their ruin (5); the Iceni, of whom the *Coitanni* were a part, were one of thefe ftates. And the limits of thefe laft, the *Coitanni*, may defervedly become the object, in this differtation, of particular confideration. Now as to the German ocean, nothing needs be faid in refpect of that, and the border towards the Cenomanni has been noted before, wherefore the boundaries of this ftate in regard of the

(1) Col. 1227. 1247.
(2) Account of Richard of Cirencefter, p. 19.
(3) Camden, col. xix.
(4) Tacitus.
(5) Camden, col. liv. from Tacitus.

Brigantes

Brigantes and Carnabii, where what is now called the county of Derby lies, requires only to be inveſtigated.

But before I touch upon the boundaries in reſpect of the Brigantes and Carnabii, I would beg leave to add a word more concerning the Iceni. The Cenomanni and the Iceni, it ſeems, were the ſame people; that is, Iceni was the generical name, and the two clans of which this people conſiſted, were called Cenomanni and Coitanni; the former lying ſouth of the river Avon, and the latter north of it. Wherefore as we find a people of the ſame name, Cenomanni, in Gaul (1), to wit, Le pays du Maine (2), one has all the reaſon in the world to imagine our Iceni were of Gauliſh extraction. However, this diſcovery of the identity of the two people very happily puts an end to the doubts of Mr. Camden; "I have long been "of opinion, ſays he, that by a mangling of the "name *Iceni*, the very ſame people were called in "*Cæſar Cenimagni*. To which I was induced, as "by the affinity of the names *Iceni* and *Cenimagni*, "ſo by comparing *Cæſar* and *Tacitus* together. For "the latter tells us, that the *Cenimagni* ſurrendered "themſelves to the Romans: now that the *Iceni* did ſo, "*Tacitus* informs us in theſe words, *on their own accord*, "*they came over to our ſide* (3). There appears not to me any mangling of the name *Iceni*, but the contrary; for from Cenimagni, expreſſed I preſume *y cenimagni*,

---
(1) Cæſar de B. G. vii. § 69.
(2) So Dr. Clarke in his Cæſar, and Cellarius, i. p. 131.
(3) Camden, col. 433.

the shorter name of *Iceni* seems to have sprung; which entirely overthrows Sir Henry Spelman's etymology of the *Iceni* from the river *Ise*, as likewise that of Mr. Camden from the *wedgy* figure of the country (1). Mr. Camden goes on: "But what is of greatest moment in "this matter, is, that a manuscript divides the word "*Cenimagni*, and reads it, *Ceni*, *Agni*; for which I "would willingly put *Iceni*, *Regni*, if it might be done "without the imputation of too great liberty. Thus "much is certain, that you will never find the *Ceni-* "*magni* in any other part of Britain, if you make them "a distinct people from the *Regni* and *Iceni*." This is very just, for the *Cenimagni* were not distinct from the *Iceni*, but actually a part of them; but then they had nothing to do with the *Regni*, or the people of Surrey and Sussex, and the reading *Ceni*, *Agni* was rather a corruption of *Cenimagni*, than of *Iceni*, *Regni*.

I proceed now upon the boundaries of the *Coitanni* in respect of the *Brigantes* and *Carnabii*. The observation of bishop Gibson is, that the bounds of the antient nations inhabiting Britain cannot be nicely determined. "For, says he, how can we hope *exactly* to distinguish "them, when our antient authors only deliver at large "in what *quarter* of the nation they were seated, "without descending to their particular limits? Be- "sides, most of the barbarous nations seem (according "to their strength at different times) to have had domi- "nions larger and narrower: especially in Britain "(where were so many kings) we cannot imagine, but

(1) Camden, col. 433.

S. "that

"that they were frequently making encroachments one
"upon another (1)". This seems to be so very reasonable, that one cannot but assent to it, and therefore, whilst I am under the influence of this persuasion, I cannot pretend to determine absolutely the boundaries of the *Coitanni*, but only to mention such as appear to be rational and plausible. Now the surest way seems to be to look out for certain natural objects for the limits of the countries in question, such as mountains and rivers; and, on inspecting Richard's antient map, the æstuary of *Abus*, or the Humber, first offers itself. Speaking of the *Abus*, or the station there, in his book, Richard says, " unde transis in Maximam ad Petuari-
"am (2)", meaning by *Maxima* the province so called by the Romans, where the *Brigantes* were seated; and accordingly he makes the distance six miles from the station called *Abus*, and the station on the opposite shore called *Petuaria*. From thence I judge the *Danus*, or the river Donne, became the boundary westward; for the station eighteen miles south of *Legeolium*, or Casterford, Richard expresly says was *Ad Fines* (3), by which must be meant the Fines *Brigantes inter et Coritanos*, as is not improperly added by Dr. Stukeley, though those words are not in the author. The boundary after this, and more westerly, seems to have been that mountainous country which stretches between the Donne and the *Seteia*, or the river Mersey, and after-

(1) Bishop Gibson in Camden, col. 433.
(2) Richard of Cirencester, p. 40.
(3) Ibid.

wards

THE CORITANI.

wards the Mersey itself. This chain of rivers and mountains, which I presume continued afterwards to be the march or limits between the kingdoms of Mercia and Northumberland, seems to have been a sufficient security against the mutual encroachments of the *Brigantes* and *Coitanni*; and that this was really the limits of the kingdom of Mercia, in the after times, might be easily shewn.

As to the *Carnabii*; the rivers Dove and Goit, which now part Derbyshire from Staffordshire, seem to have been the natural boundary of the *Coitanni* this way. Dr. Plot indeed has endeavoured to shew, that a people of the name of *Iceni* was settled in Worcestershire and Staffordshire; but this opinion I strenuously oppose, and shall reply to his arguments in order. First, he says, Tacitus mentions a British people hereabouts that were called *Iceni*, who took distaste at the Proprætor Ostorius Scapula's blocking up their countrymen between the rivers *Antona* and *Sabrina* (1), and, therefore, he suspects they belonged in part to this place, for that the *Simeni* of Norfolk, &c. whom Mr. Camden would have to be the only *Iceni*, seem to be too remote to be concerned at such an action. This argument he further inforces by observing, that the river Nen cannot well be the *Antona* of Tacitus, as both Sir Henry Savil (2), and Mr. Camden (3), would have it; he

---

(1) Tacitus, Annal. XII. c. 31.
(2) Sir Henry Savil's Translation of the Twelfth Book of Tacitus's Annals § 8.
(3) In Northamptonshire.

think's

thinks this name may be a corruption, through frequent transcribing, for one of the *Avona's*, betwixt which and the Severn they might easily be cooped up, but not so betwixt it and the River Nen, which is so far from joining it, that it holds a quite contrary course (1). Now, in answer to this, I would note, that both Ptolemy and Richard place the *Carnabii* in Staffordshire; the latter expresly mentions *Etocetum*, or Wall by Litchfield, as inhabited by the *Carnabii* (2); and, in his map, he as evidently places the *Carnabii* in Cheshire.

The *Iceni*, who took distaste at the proceeding of Ostorius, were not the *Cenimanni*, or the *Iceni* of Norfolk, &c. who, as the doctor observes, lived at too great a distance to take umbrage at such a step, but the *Coitanni*, or the *Iceni* of these more northern parts. The *Antona* of Tacitus is doubtless a corruption of *Aufona*, for so Richard writes the name of the river that runs by Northampton both in his map and elsewhere; and there is no difficulty in conceiving how Ostorius, supposing him to be north of Northampton, should hinder the *Iceni* of Norfolk, &c. from joining the *Coitanni*, and excluding them from such junction by means of the *Aufona* and Severn.

The Doctor's second argument is, that it is probable these *Iceni* were neighbours to the *Congi* or *Cangi*, against whom the Roman army was presently led after the defeat of the *Iceni*, whose territories reached, as Tacitus himself also confesses, almost to the Irish

(1) Dr. Plot's Nat. Hist. of Staff. p. 392.
(2) Page 94.

sea;

that it carries its name any further. Wherefore should any one dislike the notion last mentioned, of its being denominated from the people it passed through, they may possibly acquiesce in the *terminus ad quem*, or the country to which it led; a supposition very natural, admitting the road might be afterwards carried on further northward, for this is directly the case with the other Ikenild-street, which passing from London to the *Iceni* of Norfolk, was for that reason called the Ikenild-street.

I have all along supposed in this little debate, that the *Iceni* intended by Tacitus were those of the northern parts, otherwise known by the name of *Coitanni*, which makes it necessary for me to take notice of the following objection. The *Iceni*, whom Tacitus mentions, must, in appearance, be the same with those of Norfolk, &c. for in the same place he speaks of *a colony* of veterans posted at *Camalodunum* (a city of the *Trinobantes*, next neighbours to the *Iceni* of Norfolk, &c.) to repress the rebel Britons upon all occasions, which were drawn out at that time against the *Silures*. To this difficulty Dr. Plot replies, there were two *Camalodunums*, one in the country of the *Trinobantes*, and another in the territories of the *Cornavii* or *Cangi*, about the south part of Cheshire, whence he might much more probably draw out these veteran soldiers, being much nearer to the *Silures*, than from the *Camalodunum* of the *Trinobantes*. But this I doubt is an insufficient answer; Ptolemy very clearly places this other *Camulodunum* amongst the *Brigantes*, and not amongst sea (1); wherein in a manner he comes up to Ptolemy, who places the Καγκανῶν ἄκρον, or *Promontorium Gan-ganorum*, at Omeshead-Point, or Lheyn Gogarth, in Caernarvonshire: the *Cangi* in all likelihood also held all Denbighshire, and a piece of Cheshire, where the old *Condate*, now Congleton, and Conghull, seem to preserve the memory of them. I answer, the *Iceni*, meaning by them the *Coitanni*, one part of whom inhabited the county of Derby, were certainly near enough to the *Cangi*, for Ostorius to lead his army, after the defeat of the *Iceni*, against them.

But the capital argument, thirdly, runs thus: The Roman consular way, which remains to this hour, passes through both Worcestershire and Staffordshire, by the name of Ikenild-street, which how it should come by, but from the people, whose territories it was made through, he cannot imagine. But, with submission to this very learned man, there is no necessity for a road to take its name from the country it passes through; the case is not so with the Watling street, the Fosse, and the Ermin-street; and as to the Ikenild-street in particular, supposing it to derive its name, as he suggests, from the region it traversed, there is yet no occasion to imagine it to be borrowed from any *Iceni* in Worcestershire or Staffordshire, since it might just as well take it from the *Iceni*, or *Coitanni*, in Derbyshire. It may be of weight perhaps, to observe, that this road comes through Staffordshire, and then enters the *Iceni*, or *Coitanni*, with whom it terminates, for I cannot learn

(1) Tacitus, Annal. XII. c. 32.

that

www.ingramcontent.com/pod-product-compliance
Lightning Source LLC
Chambersburg PA
CBHW020058170426
43199CB00009B/323

the *Cornavii* or *Cangi*; for which reason Mr. Baxter very justly looks for it amongst that people, taking it to be Old Malton (1), as Dr. Gale esteems it to be more truly Almonbury (2); otherwise called *Cambodunum*. It is very plain to me that *Cambodunum*, and *Camulodunum*, are the same place, though Mr. Baxter is so desirous of making them different (3); for what Ptolemy and the geographer of Ravenna called by the latter name, Richard of Cirencester calls by the first (4). Besides, Tacitus calls the place *a colony*, which plainly indicates the *Camalodunum* of the *Trinobantes*, the other *Camulodunum* not enjoying that honour. I would, therefore, rather say, that this objection is of no weight, since the veterans of the colony at *Camulodunum* of the *Trinobantes* might be drawn out from thence against the *Silures*, which lay almost in a strait line from them, whilst Osterius was warring against the *Iceni* north of the *Ausona*, and the *Cangi*. I therefore conclude, this objection notwithstanding, that the *Iceni* here meant were the northern *Iceni* or the *Coitanni*; and, in regard to Dr. Plot, that there were no *Iceni* either in Staffordshire or Worcestershire.

(1) Baxteri Gloss. p. 64.
(2) Gale in his edition of the geographer of Ravenna.
(3) Gloss. p. 62. and 64.
(4) Richard of Cirencester, p. 27.

N. B. *In the* Addenda *to the* Dissertation on the Coins of Cunobelin, p. 111. Class V. d. *where it is said that the* Griffin *is sacred to* Mars; *add*, not only to *Mars*, but to *Apollo* also, as appears from Montfaucon, Antiq. passim, and from Spanheim, De usu & præstant. Num. vol. I. ed. fol. p. 270, 271, 272. — And that the latter deity was in high esteem with Cunobelin, is remarked above, p. 43. 80. 93.

F I N I S.